After the Gardeners' Bothy

Arthur Hooper enjoying his retirement in the gardens of Red Oaks at Henfield in V Sussex in 2000.

After the Gardeners' Bothy

Arthur Hooper

MALTHOUSE PRESS, SUFFOLK
2004

First published by Malthouse Press, Suffolk, 2004

ISBN 0 9539680 1 4

British Library Cataloguing-in-Publication Data

A catalogue record for this book is available from the British Library.

Designed by Robert Malster
Typeset by John Walton
Printed in Great Britain by
PrintWright, Ipswich

Contents

Woodcuts by Jill Goffe
Photographs from the author's collection

Foreword

DAD'S first book, *Life in the Gardeners' Bothy,* was published while he was living at the Gardeners' Royal Benevolent Society's retirement home at Henfield, Sussex. He was surprised how well it sold – surprised that his 'ordinary' experiences could be of interest to others. Then he was being asked about the rest of his life. A couple of pages at the end of the book couldn't begin to cover almost forty years of gardening life.

At ninety-one, Dad was unsure whether he had the energy to pick up his pen once more. An attack of bronchitis left him very low and, as a kind of therapy, his daughter-in-law Barbara encouraged him to write again. The more he wrote, the stronger he became, and this book is the result. After a short illness, Dad died in July 2002 at ninety-three, but not before the rest of his story had been set down.

The number of great houses of the kind he describes has diminished considerably, but they are part of our social landscape and it is important that personal experiences are recorded. We have had the opportunity to live in some wonderful places and Dad encouraged us all to appreciate what we saw. 'Just look at that,' he would say about a flower cupped in his hand. His work is still evident in the planting he did at Tyntesfield, St. Pauls Walden and other gardens he tended.

One of the last visits he made, in May 2002, was to Burghley House, Stamford, seat of the Cecil family. He was delighted

Enjoying a private tour of the gardens of Burghley House, Arthur Hooper chats to Head Gardener Richard Allam about his first book, *Life in the Gardeners' Bothy*.

to tour the private gardens with the Head Gardener, Richard Allam, and, of course, to see that the great gardens of England were in the capable hands of the next generation of gardeners.

Edwin and John Hooper

'Head Gardener, Umpire He,
Given out on 93'

Headstone epitaph, Arthur Hooper

On a visit to his son John's home at Wilbarston, near Market Harborough, in May, 2002, Arthur relaxes among the plants.

Introduction

AT THE early age of fourteen I decided I wanted to be a gardener; there then followed three years of intensive training in the glasshouses and pleasure gardens under my father, who was Head Gardener to Sir C.H.E. Chubb, the man who bought Stonehenge at an auction for £6,600 and then gave it to the nation. After three years with my father I was moved into another stately home, Fonthill House, where the Head Gardener was Mr. Mills. At Fonthill I was to live in the garden bothy with three other trainees, as I described in my earlier book *Life in the Gardeners' Bothy*.

Most stately homes had a garden bothy, situated in the garden to provide a residence for unmarried young men who were training to become the Head Gardeners of the future. We lived together as a unit, doing everything for ourselves except for the cooking of the midday meals; on working days a lady who was always called 'Mum' was employed to come in and cook our midday meal. She also attended to the bed linen and would usually do our personal washing, but it was for us to recompense her in some way.

The bothy boys were on call by the Head Gardener at any time, day or night. Bothies had strict rules, the most important being that no female might cross the threshold (except 'Mum'). Breaking this rule meant instant dismissal. Nobody might enter the bothy if any one of us objected to that person. A rota was arranged and each member of this little community took it in turn to attend to the washing up, to light the cooking range each morning, remove the ashes and carry out general chores around the bothy. The Head Gardener would appoint one of us, usually a foreman in one part of the garden, as bothy foreman. He would be responsible for buying any food we needed, the cost being shared equally. As foreman he was in charge of all that happened in the bothy.

We were classed as first journeymen, second journeymen, or even third, according to our experience. The Head might move us up a grade if he thought fit, or transfer us to to a higher grade in some other garden. Head Gardeners would probably make these transactions at a meeting in the Ranelagh Bar at the Chelsea Flower Show, where many gardeners met to exchange information on their gardens, and to discuss the movement of men to suit other Heads. They would also meet tradespeople who would often have information to pass on about job vacancies and movements of men around the various gardens. Thus it was that I moved several times from bothy to bothy during my training.

At the age of twenty-five I was rather too young to expect a Headship and, wishing to marry my fiancée, I decided to look for a married General Foreman's or Deputy Head's situation to gain experience in handling staff and working close to a Head Gardener. I found what I was seeking in the gardens of Alderbrook Park, near Cranleigh in Surrey.

Alderbrook Park   1

DOROTHY AND I married on 10th February, 1934, at St. Thomas's Church, Salisbury. That evening, after the wedding breakfast, we went to our new home in the Gardens at Alderbrook Park. I had to start work in my new job on the 12th.

We had ordered our furniture from a Salisbury firm, at a cost of just £100. This was to furnish a two-bedroomed house with sitting room, dining room and kitchen. Our three-piece suite cost £13 10s. 0d., and Dorothy's £22 bought all the bedding, towels, etc., so we had completely furnished our new home before the wedding.

At that stage Dorothy had not even seen the house which was to be her home. It was a very good house, but the water was a problem as the pipes leading to the gardens were furred up, so we were supplied with a 16-gallon water cart, brought to the house each morning by two of my men.

My job was foreman in the many glasshouses, with a staff of three. I also had to do the floral decorations in the 'big house'. Our Head Gardener, Mr. Foot, was quite elderly, so he just supervised, which meant he needed good foremen to support him.

It was in the mansion that I met our employer, a Mr. Chettle, and his wife. He had been a tea merchant in India for many years, coming back to England a rather sick but wealthy man.

Our hours were from 7am until 5pm, and I was well satisfied with that. In my charge were two carnation houses, three houses for melons and cucumbers, five peach and nectarine houses, two for tomatoes, four for plants, a large flowering house, a rose house and an alpine cool house. All the glass was in three long ranges; two ranges were span roof and the other was a lean-to which was part of the kitchen garden wall. My bothy training was now standing me in good stead, all went well and Mr. Foot seemed quite happy to give me my wages of £2 per week, with vegetables, fruit, lighting and coal, plus the free house.

I had seen one of the smaller houses with tomatoes in full fruit, which was rather unusual for February. The plants were suffering from lack of light, which was to be expected at that time of the year. Upon enquiring from Mr. Foot, I was told that Mr. Chettle always wanted to pick a tomato on Christmas Day, so it was arranged that he should be able to do so. It was plain to me that the cost of those few plants being able to produce ripe fruits so early in the year must have been quite high. I often wondered if we could ever work out the cost but, with so many other plants growing, we rather gave up trying to come up with an answer.

There was a limited amount of entertaining in the mansion and on those occasions Mr. & Mrs. Chettle's two daughters acted on their parents' behalf. They would wish the floral decorations to be quite impressive, and I enjoyed helping them with the flowers and plants on these occasions. As time went on, Mr. Foot left his three foremen to practise their own ideas, so it became necessary for Fred in the pleasure grounds, Charles in the kitchen garden and myself to work closer together as a team. I was happy with this arrangement, because it gave me more responsibility, and that would help me in due time to become a Head Gardener. Working together helped me more than it did Fred and Charles, as they were content to stay as foremen in that garden.

As the months went by Dorothy and I were very happy together. Then, in the early autumn, our doctor confirmed that Dorothy was to have a baby, which made us even happier, if at the same time a little apprehensive. When a little later on we were assured that all was well our joy was complete. We could now look forward to something very special and start preparing for the life in our care.

Our parents, too, were delighted for us, so we arranged to spend the coming Christmas in Salisbury with my people. We also spent a lot of time with Dorothy's parents, and were pleased we did so as in March her father became very ill. He died after being ill for no more than a few days. That hurt more than a little, as he had

Arthur and Dorothy on their wedding day, 10th February, 1934.

been so looking forward to his new grandchild. We had this new life coming, which was in a way a comfort to us. Even in those circumstances Dorothy's mother expressed a wish to be with us when the child was born; we were so pleased to know that Grandma would be around at that important time.

In early May King George V would be celebrating his Silver Jubilee and all around the country, on hilltops and in prominent positions, beacons would be lit. Pitch Hill, which was very close to Alderbrook Park, was to be one of the sites and everyone was keen to go to the top of the hill to see the big bonfire lit. The hill is very steep and rather difficult to climb, but my Dorothy insisted that she was going to the top! At that stage it did not seem to be a very good idea, but she was not going to be denied being there, so three of us men on the estate decided to help in any way we could.

It was not very difficult getting her to the top; however, when it came to getting her down, we had a real problem. I walked immediately in front of her and, step by step, we slowly made it down with great care, my two helpers each taking an arm. Dorothy was very thankful and happy to have succeeded, so we went into the local hostelry for some refreshments before going home.

This occasion was not the only one on which Dorothy caused concern. Another time she wanted to see a film in Cranleigh cinema, which would mean a four-mile return walk. We knew her time was close, but that film she must see, and of course she did! Then things began to happen sooner than expected, and our little son was born on 13th May, 1935. I had called the midwife, who was with Dorothy when the child made his way into the world, but, like all Dads at that time, I was not allowed to be anywhere near my wife. I went to the Post Office and sent a telegram to my mother-in-law to come as soon as possible. Not many people had a telephone, so we had to go to the Post Office and hand in the written message we wished to send, with the address to which it was to be delivered. The message would be telegraphed to the nearest main Post Office, where a telegraph boy would get on his bike and take the message to the address given. There he had to wait to see if there would be a reply; if there was, he would take it back to his office and it would be telegraphed back to the office from which the original message had come. One might have to wait an hour for a reply, but for those days that was a very quick service.

Now I knew that Grandma would be in Guildford to catch the afternoon bus to Cranleigh and that it would pass the end of our drive to Alderbrook, so she could alight there. When I left home to meet Dorothy's mother it was very cold and snowing a little, but she arrived safely. As she and I walked the long drive the weather worsened, so that by the time we arrived at the house we were both wet and cold.

That being 13th May, the weather caused a disaster to our plants in the garden. Back in the boiler house the fires were on full blast, but that did not save the plants outside. That night we registered 12°F of frost, so next morning the damage was only too apparent. The potatoes were a complete loss, as was almost all the fruit. The trees and shrubs would recover in a year or two, but it was a sad sight everywhere.

That was the worst spring, if one could call it so, in the memory of many of the older people in Cranleigh. I well remember that later in the year we picked all the fruit in a 12lb chip basket, but we did have some potatoes. We had planted about 20lb of potatoes instead of cooking them, and they gave us a yield of over 150lb when we lifted them in September.

The weather had to improve before our little son could be left outside in his Marmet pram for part of the day. Nevertheless, it did improve, and all went well until a fire started on the heath perhaps a quarter of a mile from our house. It was not long before it got a little too close for comfort, so little Edwin was kept in for a day or two because of the smoke and smuts.

He was getting on very well, so we could go for long walks with him in his pram. We had heard of what was known as the Silent Pool, very near Shere village, and we intended to see it. It was a walk of four or five miles but, with a picnic and anything else we might need in the pram, plus our baby, we set off in good weather on a Sunday morning. When we got to the pool we discovered why it was called the Silent Pool; although there was a little breeze blowing, there was no movement in the water. It seems the lay of the land had something to do with it.

We enjoyed our day out, so we decided to do it again. The next time we went to Abinger Hammer. Once more, it was a long walk, but one which we considered well worth the effort.

Ford Manor 2

IN THE autumn of that year Mr. Chettle died, and we knew this would mean very big changes. In his will he had left instructions that everyone with two years' service should have one month's wages plus a month's money for every year over two years. I had been at Alderbrook Park for one year and eleven months on his death, so I did not qualify to receive anything from the will.

Mr. Foot advised me to look for another job, and gave me a very good reference to help me in my quest. I replied to an advertisement in the *Gardener's Chronicle*, and Mr. Gooden, Head Gardener at Ford Manor, asked me to go on interview. I knew Ford Manor was a very important garden near Lingfield in Surrey, so I lost no time getting to see Mr. Gooden. It was a good interview as he offered me the post as his deputy, living in one of the lodge cottages.

I was more than glad to accept, and when I told my wife she was delighted to know we could be at Ford Manor within the month. Mr. Gooden had said he would pay for our move, for which we were thankful. From the career point of view this was a good move, because having a job as a deputy Head would help me on to a Headship later.

The cottage stood at the entrance to the Manor, where there was a gate which was closed to everyone on Good Friday. Dorothy and I saw to it that nobody passed through the gate unless their business was important, like perhaps the postman. This was done to ensure that the driveway was kept private at all times. Near the cottage was a kitchen garden, and passing between my house and the vegetable garden was a small stream in which there were many minnows.

As one of the benefits of my new employment I was to have one barrowful of coal brought to our house every working day, and vegetables from the garden as needed, which did not amount to very much as the cottage had its own garden where we could, and did, grow a lot of our needs. There was a second kitchen garden a little way off where hardy fruit trees grew on a long wall— peaches, cherries, nectarines and figs. There were also many fruit bushes, together with a number of garden frames in which were lettuce, endive, radish, and even melons. Other frames were set aside for bedding plants and other flowers being grown on for planting in the pleasure garden.

Most of the land was given over to main crop potatoes and almost all members of the cabbage family, then in due time the two gardens reversed the crops. The ranges of glass and six span houses were quite near the Manor, and in a way they merged into

Mr. Gooden pointing proudly to the *Lilium giganteum* in the Ford Manor gardens, which were the gardeners' pride and joy.

the pleasure garden, passing through the Sarcophagus Dell, so called because of the two tombs, though I gathered they were in fact no more than garden ornaments.

Mr. Gooden called me to his office that first morning in order that we could have a long talk. In the 1914–18 War he had suffered a leg wound which did trouble him at times, so he wanted me to do the running about, to see that the men were all right in their work and that they were carrying out their orders. Five men were employed in the pleasure garden, four in the kitchen gardens and four under glass, the two boys being moved around as needed.

I found working under Mr. Gooden more of a pleasure than a job; it was no hardship at all to do all he asked of me, the time factor never came into my mind. It was another pleasure when my Dorothy and Mrs. Gooden became good friends, so my small son had almost two mothers.

As time went by I found my work becoming even more interesting. We had a collection of rare daffodils, and any new varieties were sent to us for trial, so each spring there was something new to see. We were propagating many kinds of plants for use in the extensive garden, which was still being enlarged. Plants which would give good colour for a long period were planted around the Manor, while others which were of particular interest were to be found in various parts of the pleasure gardens, including a collection of *Liliums*. The pride and joy of the gardeners were the *Lilium giganteum*, which would often grow to a height of eight feet, with each stem having up to ten highly scented white flowers. Although one could hardly reach the lower blooms, the scent around the plants was at times quite overpowering. It might take as long as three years for a young bulb to reach the flowering stage, but it was so worthwhile in order to see these spectacular plants in flower.

Ford Manor was the home of Colonel and Mrs. Clay. Colonel Clay was the Member of Parliament for Tunbridge Wells and an important member of the government, and Mrs. Clay was a member of the Astor family, her sister Nancy being the first woman M.P. That being so, many important people were guests in the house, so the garden had to be of a high standard. Mr. Gooden was the type of Head Gardener to take charge of a garden of importance like Ford Manor. I had had a good gardening training during my years in bothies, but now I was being enlightened in those other skills of management and employment of labour.

We had been in the lodge cottage for less than a year when we were moved into a flat so as to be near the glasshouses and, of course, the boilers. The flat, over a recently closed laundry, was quite spacious, so there was plenty of room for our little son to ride around on his three-wheeled cycle. Part of the next-door flat was built over the archway leading into this part of the garden. We had a middle-aged couple, Sid the estate carter and his wife, as neighbours. Sid's pride and joy were his four lovely grey heavy horses, which were a splendid sight when they were working, their harnesses immaculate and their brasses shining. Sid would be seen walking in front of his team, whip (which was never used) held high in the air.

Sid and his horses were a feature of our estate; out of date, maybe, but so well worth keeping. One day Sid told me he was expecting a baby. Perhaps I may have looked a little surprised, for he said "Not my wife, but Rosie, one of my mares." He asked me if I would give him some help if it was needed when the time came, and I was only too happy to agree. As the day came nearer Sid asked me if I would feed Rosie sometimes so that she would become used to seeing me in her stall.

Sid set aside part of the stable block as a maternity unit. It was cleaned and disinfected, and new, clean straw was brought in, so almost everything was ready. When the time came there was very little to do as everything went so very well, and the filly was born without needing any help. We had hot water in two buckets which was needed for a time as a little cleaning up was necessary, then we left mother and child together. It was surprising how quickly the baby was on her feet. Sid allowed no visitors that day, but the next day Colonel and Mrs. Clay came down and named the new-born Rosebud. We were not best pleased with this new name, but it had to stay. A few visitors did see Rosebud that day, but Sid did not encourage visitors as he did not want Rosie to be worried by having too many people in the stable for a few days.

Ford Manor was an important garden in the horticultural world, but it had no garden bothy. All the labour was local, most of the workers living in the nearby village of Dormansland. At times, if there was a sudden change in the weather, the greenhouse duty men would have to come quickly to attend to the boilers but, as I was living in the garden, I would often see what was happening and take any action needed before the men could arrive, proving again what an asset was the garden bothy.

Thinning bunches of grapes is a skill greenhouse workers should perfect. Mr. Gooden and I were so engaged one day when Mrs. Clay and Lady Astor came through into the vineries, and the two sisters stopped to watch. Lady Astor said to Mr. Gooden something like "You do know what you are doing?" His reply was "If someone can teach me anything to do with my profession, I'll be most attentive." The two ladies went on their way.

We had the honour of a visit by the Queen of Romania, who came to see English floral art at a stately home. She stayed for nearly three weeks, watching and helping Mrs. Clay. However, there were times when Madam was called away and would leave the Queen and me to complete the particular item we were doing. I felt it a great privilege to have been in the company of that gracious lady.

It was in January, 1936, that the BBC told us of the death of King George V, and it was announced that the then Prince of Wales was now King Edward VIII. This was no surprise, as we had been informed the previous day that the King was very ill. Also in that same news bulletin were disturbing reports of the doings of Adolf Hitler and his government in Germany. Dorothy and I liked to listen to the wireless, nowadays called radio, in the evenings when our son was asleep in his cot. Some of the programmes were very good—nice music, entertaining humour, a lot of the doings of the new King, but always that man Hitler was reported for something he had done or said. Tommy Handley had a programme on the wireless called *ITMA* (It's That Man Again), in which he made a mockery of Hitler and his actions. It was very funny and popular, and at least it gave us a laugh, which was more than could be said for Hitler and his doings.

Late June was the time when we took cuttings of shrubs and other hardy plants. Mr. Gooden chose a dull, rainy day to collect the many cuttings we would need to propagate in order to keep up the supply of plants needed to renew and enlarge the ever-growing garden at Ford Manor. Mr. Gooden took no labels, so the cuttings we collected became all mixed up, but when we returned to the potting shed he was able to identify each species and variety, then to label them. I learned a great deal about identification of plants by their leaves that day.

Later that year our sunken garden was a vista of colour when a plant, *Tropaeolum speciosum*, took over the whole garden, covering all the herbaceous plants with its bright scarlet flowers. Fortunately it does little damage to other plants because it grows rather late in the summer and its hosts are starting to die back.

One day in early December the butler asked Mr. Gooden if we could put on a good dining table decoration as some very important people would be the guests, perhaps around twenty people, so our flowers would need to be spread over the length of the table. We were happy to do this, using carnations, chrysanthemums, and some forced bulbs, with fern and trailing ivy. We did see some of the guests arrive; Mr. Stanley Baldwin was one, but this was not unusual as he was a frequent visitor to Ford Manor. The next day a young footman who had been waiting at table and had overheard conversation during the dinner started to talk.

Fortunately one of the first people to whom he spoke was our Mr. Gooden, who quickly stopped him speaking and told him he was betraying confidential information, but unfortunately he had already said too much. The information was startling: it appeared the King might possibly abdicate. Whether the abdication crisis was the reason for this gathering or the matter had merely come up during the dinner-table discussion we had no way of knowing, but it seemed to us that the matter might well be a state secret and that we would be wise to forget what we had heard.

Mr. Gooden called all his staff together and told us in no uncertain way to keep our thoughts unspoken. What happened to that young footman we never knew, but he was not seen again at Ford Manor. Just three days later the King really knew he was going, for on 11th December he signed a document of abdication. During that same week he made a broadcast on the wireless, telling the nation that he could not continue as King without the help and support of the lady whom he loved, so he was making way for his brother. The Duke of York would now be King George VI, and he and the Duchess of York were crowned King George VI and Queen Elizabeth on 12th May, 1937.

Our son was growing fast, and I was thirty, so once again becoming a Head Gardener was very much in my mind. Dorothy, too, said it would be nice to be a Head's wife. I talked the matter over with Mr. Gooden, and he advised me to be patient and wait until the right situation came along.

The spectacular rock garden of Hookstile House, of which the owners, Mr. and Mrs. Horner, were justifiably proud.

Hookstile House

IT WAS not until July, 1939, that I had an interview with Mr. and Mrs. Horner at Hookstile House in Godstone, some 14 miles south of Croydon in Surrey. I liked what I had seen in the garden, they seemed to be happy with me, and by the time I left after my interview I had my first Head's appointment.

The house in which we were to live had only recently been built. At that stage it had no garden, though there was plenty of space around the house to develop one. Dorothy had been over to Hookstile and was very pleased with all that she had seen, and Mr. Gooden said he needed no notice from me, so we moved into our new home in mid-July.

I had only three men working for me, which was enough for a garden of that size. There was not a great deal of glass, a very good kitchen garden, but Mr. and Mrs. Horner's pride and joy was the superb rock garden. They had collected a number of plants on their journeys abroad, some of which I had never seen, so now I had to learn from experience, no longer relying on other people.

Mr. Horner's main interest was riding. He kept two horses in the stable and most days went riding with his groom mounted on the spare horse. He also spent a lot of time in the garden, as did Mrs. Horner, who generally had one or two of her three girls with her. The youngest was most of the time with Nanny, who cared for the six-year-old.

There were four other cottages on the estate; the groom lived in one on his own, the butler and his wife in another, and two of my men, John Welling and Charlie Brough, with their wives made up the small community. Fred Withum, my other man, lived in Godstone.

During those first weeks all seemed to be going so well, but of course it did not last. There was now some very serious trouble with Hitler and his German army; it looked as though there might well be war. Our Government had decided to evacuate the children from London and other large cities and towns, and we in the country were to accept these children into our homes. I can't say we were happy with these arrangements but, if war did come, these children must be kept free from danger, therefore it was up to us to take the young people in and try to care for them and keep them happy. We were to be paid to do this service, so we could hardly complain.

It was quite late one evening when the Evacuation Officer brought two ten-year-old girls to our door. These girls were to be in our care; they were both very tired as they had left London in the morning and had been from place to place with their school friends who had been dropped off, one or two at a time, with people whom they didn't know. These girls were strangers to us, and we to them. My Dorothy very quickly gave them something to eat and put them together in our spare bed. After settling them, she came down with some of their clothes. She looked at the clothes and knew she had made a mistake, as they were not as clean as she would have expected. She had only given the girls a quick wash before putting them in bed so, as they appeared to be asleep when we looked in on them later, we would have to see to their needs in the morning. They did look better by daylight, except that their hair needed attention. Dorothy washed their hair and combed it through carefully, but the young people thought it was quite unnecessary when we went to make their bed. To our horror there were marks on the sheet which, we were sure, were flea marks. All the bedding was bundled up and put out on the drying line, where it stayed all day. Fortunately the weather kept dry.

Mrs. Horner saw the clothes on the line and wanted to know why they were there. I had to tell her everything, the more so because of our little son and the need to keep him clean. She took the two girls into the 'big house', and later we gathered they were bathed and dressed in clothes which her two eldest girls no longer needed. When they came back to us they were very changed young ladies, and so proud of their new outfits. Clare, the elder of the two, was very much the leader, often answering for Doris, who was much more reserved. The families of our girls must have been informed where their daughters were staying, as the following Sunday the mothers and fathers of the girls arrived at our house in a very second-hand car. They wanted to be sure their girls were all right with us.

They introduced themselves as Mr. and Mrs. Mudd, Clare's parents, and Mr. and Mrs. Goodstall, Doris's parents. It was then we discovered that we had a small problem: we hadn't enough chairs for all to sit down, so the floor was the only answer. Doris wanted to return to London with her mother and father when our visitors were leaving, and a few tears were shed for a time. It was Clare who helped to settle Doris down, Dorothy being rejected for a while, and I seemed to be of no help at all.

One day, the farm manager asked me to tell the girls to stop chasing his sheep. When I did so, they told me they only wanted to touch them, to know if they were real sheep. When I asked the manager if the girls could visit the farm, he was only too happy for them to do so and touch real sheep, cows and pigs. The children were delighted, hardly believing these animals were real and alive. We were beginning to get a lot of pleasure from the company of these young people, even more so as they enjoyed playing with our little son, taking him for short walks and even into the village in his pushchair after they had been there with Dorothy on two occasions. Their great joy was the farm, and they wanted to show little Edwin how to touch farm animals.

The local school was now rather overcrowded with so many evacuees, and there were times when the teachers needed to show some tolerance to both local and visiting children. It took several days for the situation to return to something like normal, but things did settle down, the children playing together and forming friendships.

Things on the home front were improving, but the international scene was getting really dangerous. When Germany invaded Poland the talk was all of war, then we knew that the war we had been dreading was about to start. On 3rd September, 1939,

In the gardens of Hookstile House, which contained a number of plants collected by the owners on their overseas journeys.

our Prime Minister, Mr. Neville Chamberlain, spoke to the nation on the wireless telling us that we were now at war with the Germans, so we must keep tuned in to listen carefully to all announcements by the BBC. Dorothy and I now had something of a worry as to the likelihood of me being called into the forces and what would be best for her and Edwin if I was away for some time. The problem was solved in a very unexpected way.

One Sunday morning the sirens sounded, warning us of raiders approaching. Mrs. Horner must have panicked, because she put her three daughters in her car, along with some other items, and drove away, leaving Mr. Horner to explain her going. He told the butler that Madam was taking the children to their other house in Devon for the time being. On the Wednesday Mr. Horner drove down to Devon and we all hoped he would bring his wife back to Hookstile.

He was away almost a week, and upon his return the butler told everyone we were to see Mr. Horner in the hall. All eleven of the paid staff were gathered to see our employer, only to be told that Mrs. Horner would not return and that Mr. Horner would be going back to Devon to join her and the children. He gave every employee one month's written notice to terminate our employment, with one month's money. We were to vacate our houses as soon as possible as he intended to put Hookstile on the market immediately. Dorothy and I had now to decide how we could manage this new situation, remembering our two evacuees.

I wrote a letter to my father, explaining what had happened. Return post brought a letter from him telling me he had already lost three of his men, as they were members of the Territorial Army, and did I think I could help him out even if it was only for a short time? He suggested that we went to Salisbury to live with him and Mum until we could find a place on our own or, if I was called up, then Dorothy and our boy would be with family. Dorothy told me that at her home, also in Salisbury, there was a large back room where we could store our furniture if her mother agreed. Having written to ask, by return of post we had a letter saying she was delighted with the idea as now she would have her daughter and grandson near her.

This arrangement solved our problems, at least for a time. I had to contact the Evacuation Office to find the girls a new billet, and quickly, as we were going to have a lot of packing to do. When we told the girls they would have to move, Clare was quite upset. Doris said nothing for a time, then she too burst into tears. My wife and I were very moved, near to tears ourselves. We had come to care for these young ladies, and now we could see they had some love for us. They were taken from us, but not before they had been to the village and bought us a little stone vase as a present. Again, it was a moving moment as we bid them farewell, knowing we were unlikely ever to see them again. Sad to say, we never did.

We were able to move a week later and to store our home in my mother-in-law's backroom, as arranged. My parents prepared a bedroom for Dorothy and me, with young Edwin in another small room, so we were able to live together as a family.

War work in Salisbury 4

MY FATHER explained the new set-up to me. He was still Head Gardener at Bemerton Lodge, and also had charge of the gardens at the Old Manor. Sir Cecil Chubb, who was owner of Bemerton Lodge when my father was first employed there, had died in 1934 and the mansion had become a home for ex-servicemen who had no home of their own. The garden staff was somewhat reduced, but having charge of the Old Manor as well my father still had a staff of fourteen.

The Old Manor was a large private mental asylum, with 300 people in separate wards of about thirty in each, some male, the others female. Each ward had a garden surrounded by a high wall. The doors into the gardens, sometimes only one, sometimes two, were automatically locked at all times, as were the entrances into the wards. This was for safety reasons, as some of the patients were, or might become, dangerous to themselves or other people. The gardens were planted to give colour and interest, which was of therapeutic value to the patients.

I was to manage the five areas of kitchen garden, having a staff of only two elderly men. My main workforce was anything between six and ten patients who wished to come out from the wards to help in the garden. The men, whom I collected each morning and afternoon, were in the main ex-soldiers of the 1914–18 War who were classed as shell-shocked. They had been carefully selected for me to take into the kitchen garden, where there were no restrictions. Most of the time these fellows were quite good workers, and with my two full-time men helped by the patients we could produce a lot of good vegetables for the kitchens. We had to calculate the amount of any one vegetable needed for a meal by working out the amount for ten people, then relate that to four hundred, which included the staff.

We were granted permission to grow some plants and flowers

for the wards. Alan Randall, another ex-soldier, did the growing in the glasshouses of Llangaran, which was an annexe of the Manor. He would often give me some help, as I did him when he was moving plants into or out of the wards. In order to do his work around the asylum, Alan was provided with a master key. I only needed a key to the male wards, as that was where my men were to be found when I had to collect them for work.

Alan, or any man who had to go into the ladies' wards, had first of all to ring a push bell situated outside on the wall to announce that a man was about to enter. This would summon a nurse to meet him and stay with him all the time he was working, as some of the ladies, seeing a man, would crave his company and make a real nuisance of themselves. It happened in reverse if a lady had reason to go into the male quarters, and yet the doctors and the matron could move around without any problems from either men or women. Even so, Dr. Martin, the Medical Superintendent, was on one occasion attacked by a patient, suffering a slight cut to his head.

Dr. Carruthers, the deputy superintendent, had the help of Dr. Westrup when needed. Each ward had a Sister in charge on the ladies' side, and a Chief Attendant for the men. It took me some time to get used to working in a mental asylum, though I could see it was very well run. Gradually I felt more at ease with the patients working for me and, at times, was able to help them with their real or imagined problems.

Things seemed to be going quite well living with my parents. For the time being I and my wife and son were together, but we wondered how long this could last, with the war on everyone's minds. When would the time come when I was called up? Three months later I was officially informed that I was doing work of national importance, therefore I could not leave or change my work until the country was no longer at war; any change of address had to be notified. We were quite happy with this order, as it meant I could now stay with my wife and son.

It was not long before I did have to notify the War Office of a change of address, as I was able to rent a house not far from my work and fairly close to Dorothy's mother. We were pleased that we could now live together again in a home of our own. The day we moved in, the street Air Raid Warden came to see how many persons would be living in the house; it was his duty to know everyone in his area and to organise shelter in case of an air raid. He would make sure no lights could be seen from any house after dark to spoil the blackout, which was intended to confuse the crew of any hostile aircraft flying over so that they would not know whether they were over a town or over open country. The street lamps were never lit, car side lights were dimmed and headlights were masked so that they threw only a little light on to the road just a few yards ahead. These restrictions applied to all traffic, so it was considered sensible to wear something white if one was walking along the street. To black out one's window a heavy curtain might be adequate, but a more efficient method was a light wooden frame to fit each window, covered with blackout paper which one could buy in the shops.

Everyone was issued with a ration book to take to the shops when buying food. The coupons inside were exchanged for the food being bought, then the shopkeeper surrendered the coupons to buy in more food, thus ensuring that everyone had their proper share of rationed items and no more.

While we were sitting comfortably at home one evening the siren started to wail, warning us of a possible air raid. We sheltered under the stairs, as our street warden had advised us, until the all clear was sounded by the siren, this time by a single note. The sound of the siren was to become a familiar one to us all as time went on.

I felt that I was not doing enough for the war effort and that there must be something I could do in addition. Our warden put me in touch with a Mr. George Norris, who was a sergeant in the St. John Ambulance Brigade, and he suggested I might like to join him as first aid was going to be greatly needed if raids became more frequent. Dorothy and I talked the situation over and decided there was indeed more I could do, so I joined the St. John Ambulance Brigade.

Salisbury market-place presented a busy scene in the 1930s, just before Arthur joined his father in the gardens of the Old Manor.

As a new boy, I had to report for training two evenings a week. When I became more proficient I attended only once a week, as was the case with all members of the Brigade. It was a joy to know these men and women, they were so helpful.

It was at this time that the war became much more violent. Mr. Winston Churchill, the Prime Minister, decided to step up what was then called Air Raid Precautions (ARP). We in St. John's were drafted into ARP, and though the Brigade continued doing its own work, there was increasing emphasis on what we would do in the event of air raids; ARP was to become the main activity. Three depots were set up for first aid, X, Y and Z. I was drafted into Y and every time the siren sounded, day or night, I had to report to Y at once to be ready for action. One night each week a party of eight first-aiders had to gather together in a house where we were on duty all night. We were able to sleep, but we could shed only our outer garments so as to be ready for action at a minute's notice.

People who lived too far from a public air raid shelter were provided with an Anderson shelter, made of arched corrugated steel and partly sunk into the garden, and big enough to hold five to seven people. As our house was near a small river we were unable to have a shelter outside, so we were supplied with a Morrison indoor shelter, a steel table strong enough to withstand a major part of a house falling on to it. Underneath there was room to put a mattress for sleeping, but it would take only two adults plus two children.

On the Continent things had been going badly for our forces in the early part of 1940; March was even worse, but April and May brought disaster: Norway, Denmark, Holland and Belgium were occupied by the Germans and then in June France capitulated. It proved impossible for our army, on its own and still in France, to halt the advancing Germans; so began the epic rescue of our men from the beaches of Dunkirk in May and June, 1940. The Battle of Britain started in August and the air forces of Britain and Germany fought for mastery of the skies over southern Britain. Not having the success they expected, the Germans started all-out bombing of London and other towns and cities in England.

Late in 1940 there were major changes in ARP, the parties being enlarged to twelve people to incorporate rescue personnel. Now we all had to learn rescue work as well as first aid. In order to practice this we were taken to a place near Wilton where some houses had been demolished, and there we were required to rescue some casualties, represented by dummies. We also had to tunnel through a very large heap of debris using only materials found on site, and we did learn a great deal about how a house might collapse after an explosion.

It was in the later part of 1940 that Dorothy told me we were to have an addition to the family, which was wonderful news. Young Edwin was now five years old and had started school, which he seemed to enjoy; it gave him the opportunity to play with other children. We were rather hoping he would have a sister.

I was now working all day and spending most of my evenings doing war service, so Dorothy and I were seeing less and less of each other. She never complained, caring for our son and seeing to my needs was just a job to do. She considered herself lucky to have her husband around when so many wives had their men away, either in the forces or directed to work in a factory doing monotonous work, or even down a coal mine.

With all the bombings in England, we in ARP were now in the front line. Our training seemed likely to be put to the test, and yet the threat of air raids was not our greatest worry; invasion seemed to be imminent, as soon became apparent. In the south strongpoints were being built along most roads and railways, sea defences were constructed along the south and east coasts, all place names were removed, all signposts taken down and destroyed, names disappeared from railway stations and any name on a shop that gave a clue to its position had to be taken down or painted over. The idea was to confuse any invader who might get into the country either by land, sea or air, but sometimes others got confused as well.

On April 14th, 1941, my wife presented me with a wonderful baby daughter, Diane. She was a perfectly healthy child, bringing with her great joy to all the family. Young Edwin looked at this new baby and asked us if she was real. He was not sure, so he touched her. Then, satisfied, he wanted to go out and play and to tell his friends that now he had a sister, just as they did.

The St. John Ambulance Brigade still had to attend to the elderly and sick as well as carrying out any first aid necessary on the civil side. One evening we were called to deal with a maternity case, and there was only George and myself on duty. We picked up the young mother-to-be at a place called Breamore and brought her to our hospital in Salisbury, but they could not admit her owing to war casualties and we were told that only Lymington could take her. It was a foggy night, and with the restrictions on vehicle lighting we made rather slow progress. We were in the New Forest when our patient rang the emergency bell, so we had to stop to see if the lady was all right. It was obvious that the child was about to be born, so George had to find a place to park off the road; as it was dark, another driver might not see us.

At about 2am we had to deliver the baby. We had been told

what to do in a case like this, but doing it for real was a very different matter! With some help from the mother, the child came into my hands; George quickly wiped the new-born's nose, mouth and eyes with his handkerchief and the child cried out, so we knew he was all right.

We wrapped him in triangular bandages, though still attached to the mother. We used a number of triangular bandages to clean up after the birth and put child and mother together in blankets to keep them warm. We had been told not to cut the umbilical cord if we could get some medical help within the hour, and, as the sky was beginning to lighten, George thought he could get to Lymington in about twenty minutes. I stayed with our patient for the quarter-hour drive, at the end of which I was only too pleased for the nurse at the hospital to take over. A little later we were told we had done quite a good job, and for some time afterwards at Brigade meetings we were known as the midwives!

Stationed in the city were five barrage balloons. These were on long wire cables and could ascend to a very considerable height when the alert was sounded. Any aircraft flying below the

A street scene in Salisbury in the years before the war.

balloons might well have a wing damaged or even cut off if it fouled a cable. The purpose of the balloons was to stop planes flying low to attack selected targets. It was assumed that any enemy aircraft approaching the country would be seen and an alert would be sounded on the siren, but there were times when the system failed.

One day, I was in the garden with my men when there was an explosion nearby as two German planes flew very low over where we were working. We could hardly believe our eyes. Within minutes a huge fire was to be seen which, I realised, must be near to my home. I reported to the depot at once, leaving my men to be taken to their wards by our two employed people. On arrival at the depot I learned that the big gasholder was on fire and that I should go home at once as our house was only about sixty yards from the gasholder. I lost no time getting there. Dorothy had kept very cool, showing no fear, so the children felt safe, but her face told me quite a different story. The paint on the outside of our house and on five or six more houses had started to burn; the ARP warden already had a hose working to keep the houses a little cool. Some glass in the windows had cracked, but it did not shatter because we had put one-inch-wide sticky tape on the inside of all our windows. There were some brave firemen keeping the fire from spreading, but the gas had to burn until it was all gone. We had a restricted gas supply for a few days, but that was the least of our worries. Nobody was hurt, which was what really mattered.

The country was still in a state of tension, with an invasion always possible. When Hitler invaded Russia the tension relaxed somewhat for a little while, but German raids kept on coming so we still had to be ready for anything at any time. After a few weeks there was less air activity, but occasional raids kept us always ready for action.

Food rationing became very severe. Two ounces of butter had to last one person for a week, and most other foods were similarly restricted. Even clothes were rationed, but the children were given special foods so as not to impede their health or growth. With two children to care for and feed we were happy for our two and, as I could get fresh vegetables, we did not do too badly. Edwin was doing well at school and little Diane was growing fast; I was able to spend a little more time at home, so it seemed to us that perhaps the worst was over. However, there was a great deal more to do yet.

In the garden I now had up to twelve men at times; production was improving, which was important as there were even more patients in the asylum. The improvement was in part due to the extra land in cultivation at Bemerton Lodge, where the cricket field was taken over for vegetables, though the actual playing area was left intact. The flower garden was also given over to vegetables, giving us about two acres more land in all.

Tragedy 5

THE YEAR of the long-awaited invasion of Europe, 1944 was a momentous year in many ways, but for Dorothy and me it started very badly indeed. There had been some alerts, so I had been in the depot for several nights, but on the night of 24th January I was home, and we retired a little early.

Little Diane was restless. She tried to cry, but somehow it did not seem right. Dorothy said she would take her downstairs, telling me to catch up on some sleep.

She had only been downstairs a short time when she called out, very loudly, for me to come to her quickly. Dorothy was nursing Diane; she cried out that she did not think Diane was breathing. I took the child from her; she wasn't breathing, and I started artificial respiration. On a small child it was difficult, but try I must.

I told my wife to run to the warden's house to phone our doctor, tell him quickly the reason and ask him to hurry. My efforts seemed useless; perhaps we were in a state of panic, frantic even. The doctor arrived very quickly, placed Diane on the table and opened her throat to expose her windpipe. There was no bleeding, and I knew at that moment we had lost our lovely child.

I don't know what I said to Dorothy or what she said to me; we clung together in a stupor. The doctor said something about police, and coroner. He collected our son, saying he would take him to my parents. The warden and his wife came to give us some support and help, and stayed with us for the rest of the night.

In the morning, my mother came. She was with us at the awful time when the police came to take our Diane away. We needed to let my mother-in-law know, so I went to see her; when I told her what had happened she immediately said she must go to her daughter. I walked with her to our house, then I left mother and daughter together for a long time. When I did go in Dorothy's Mum cried on my shoulder, and I think I cried with her.

I had to contact an undertaker, so I called on Mr. Case who I knew was a friend of my Dad's. He came to see us and assured us he would see to everything. The next day the police came again, this time to ask questions. Had we given our little girl anything that might have burned her throat, or anything that might have choked her? That afternoon, more questions, and again the following morning. Four days later Diane was brought home. Mr. Case had covered her in white silk, she looked so beautiful. Dorothy and I just looked and wondered why we should lose our lovely daughter, not yet three years old, so full of life, but now asleep.

The police superintendent came to see us to apologise for his men doing what they had had to do. He spoke of people who did harm their children, that being the reason for all the questions. He gave Dorothy a kiss on the cheek and offered me his hand, which I was pleased to take.

It was surprising how many people called to offer condolences, many of them perfect strangers to us; some even brought flowers. I suppose the reason for some of this kindness was because a report had appeared in the local press. We had to say goodbye to our little lovely in the cemetery on a cold, dull day. We dismantled the cot, but even then we knew that in a few months we would need it again. Meanwhile, we still had Edwin to love and care for, so our lives still had a purpose, and we had a good reason to smile again.

I had been away from work for over a week and it was time for me to return, but I did not like my wife to be on her own when Edwin was at school. My mother-in-law suggested that she stay with us for a few weeks, an idea with which I was very happy. We took the mattress from under the Morrison table to make up her bed, even though the Germans were still active in the air. Once again, it was under the stairs for us when the siren sounded.

When Dorothy's mother did return to her own home she still came to visit most days. This was most fortuitous as, on the morning of 12th May, 1944, when I returned home for my lunch, mother-in-law and a midwife were in the house. Dorothy had prepared lunch, even though she must have been in labour. Her Mum had arrived and, when she saw that the baby was near, she had called the midwife in. When I arrived, I thought for lunch, the midwife was about to take Dorothy upstairs where preparations had already been made for delivery.

Dorothy then said "Put my lunch in the oven, I'll want it shortly". Which is what she did in the afternoon, with our new baby already born. Then I could go in to see her and our new son. It was magic; both mother and child were perfect. There was joy in my heart as I cycled up to tell my parents the wonderful news. They lost no time in coming to see their new grandchild. When Edwin was introduced to his new brother all he wanted to know, seeing his Mum in bed, was "Is she all right?" Dorothy and I had decided our new son's name was to be John Geoffrey, a name we thought with which he could grow up.

The cot was brought into use again, but this time a new pram for the child who had made us really happy again. Perhaps it was repercussions of fear, but every night when John was in his cot we both would listen, sometimes for over an hour, to make sure he was still breathing, and when he cried, what a relief! It was a long time before we admitted to each other that that is what we had both been doing.

Three weeks later there was a great deal happening around us. We had seen a number of tanks, armoured cars, troop carriers and personnel on the move, all going south. This went on for a day and two nights. In the morning of 6th June we looked up to see scores of planes, fighters and bombers, the larger planes towing gliders, all going south. Something big was happening, to be sure, but what? We knew what it was when the BBC announced that our soldiers, with the Americans, had landed on the beaches of Normandy and were progressing inland. This was great news; did it mean the war might come to an end before long? Would there be no more air raids? All these questions were in people's minds.

There was great concern for all the men fighting for us, in the air and on the ground, in that hostile land. There seemed so little we could do for those brave men who were doing so much for us. The thinking in the Brigade was that we would be ready to be called upon at any time to do first aid, or any other task that might help. The army took care of its men, so our assistance was limited in the main to doing the job for which we had trained. We rushed to every call, sometimes to do nothing really important. Road accidents needed to be attended quickly, they might be serious, and first aid was provided to the injured with great care and efficiency. With training and constant practice, we kept the high standard St. John's demanded.

The hostilities on the Continent went on for another year, and it was not until May, 1945, that Hitler committed suicide, Germany surrendered and the war in Europe ended. Then, for the first time in nearly six years, the BBC and the newspapers gave us a weather forecast; the blackout restrictions could be lifted and the street lights switched on again. All vehicles could use their lights as needed. Now after dark, with all the lights on, it seemed like fairyland, which in a way it was.

The war in the Far East continued until August, 1945, after which peace was declared and our troops could come home to a richly deserved welcome. Celebrations went on for several days. We in St. John's were invited to attend the Cathedral, in full dress, for a Thanksgiving Service attended by all religious denominations, together with the Navy, Army, Air Force and civic dignitaries.

Now that the war was over, I wanted to continue my career as a Head Gardener. I applied, therefore, to be released from my employment at the asylum but I was informed that I would have to wait until the government could assess the labour problem, with so many men being discharged from the Services. It was not until late in 1946 that I was informed I could move.

I watched the situations vacant in the *Gardener's Chronicle* and informed the major seed firms as they kept an agency for employment. These firms were very important, knowing where jobs were available and informing applicants. The service was good for future business, and helpful to gardeners.

Green End   6

IN DUE course I received a letter from Carters Seeds telling me to apply to a Mr. Hanbury at Green End House, Little Munden, near Ware in Hertfordshire, who was looking for a young, active Head Gardener. I wrote and received a reply, giving me a date for interview in the first week of 1947, and three weeks later we moved into our new home at Green End. As we were moving in, a new chauffeur was moving into the house next door; Bill Townsend was his name. It was the start of a great friendship between us and between our ladies, and I'm sure we all thought it was a good omen.

As the furniture was being moved into the two houses, Mr. and Mrs. Hanbury came to see that all was well, and asked if there was anything we needed. Then, saying that they would see us in the morning, Mr. and Mrs. Hanbury left us to our moving. It was at that point that I went to the outside toilet and found, to my dismay, that there was no water, just a bucket with a bottle of disinfectant nearby. Had I known before, it is doubtful if I would have taken the job, but as it was we would have to accept the situation. I learned later that none of the houses in Green End hamlet had a water closet, and a tanker came each week to attend to the hygiene. The mansion and farm had water closets which drained into septic tanks, and they had to be cleaned out every six months by the tankers.

The houses we occupied were part of the kitchen garden wall; some of my greenhouses were lean-tos built on to our houses, so that three windows of my house were inside two greenhouses, something which, in time, I found convenient.

Mr. Hanbury and I made a tour of the estate two days later, and went through the lean-to greenhouses on the walls of our houses. There was a run of 250 feet of glass where I could grow houseplants, carnations, melons, cucumbers, peaches, and the many other plants, in their season, which this estate would need.

The kitchen garden was a little over two acres, with a building almost in the middle serving as my office, store room and fruit room. The fruit cage for soft fruits was to the south of this building, and on the south and west walls fruit trees were trained— apples, pears, plums and peaches. Interplanted between the trees were cordon gooseberries, red currants and Worcester berries, a cross between black currants and gooseberries; the fruit was like a small black gooseberry, highly flavoured. All the fruit and the vegetables and plants under glass were in excellent condition, which said much for my predecessor (I later learned why he felt he had to move away).

There was a road separating this part from the 'big house' and the rest of the estate. The pleasure gardens were fairly extensive, about three acres of lawn, a rockery, pond, and flower beds. A herbaceous border led into a small wild garden, then on into a wood. I could see that with my three men we would be able to keep the estate to a high standard.

When I returned to the glasshouses I met my men, Stanley, Jack and Tom, who all lived in Green End hamlet. Stan and Jack were married, Tom lodged with Jack. I went home to tell my wife of all that I had seen, then she and I set about making our home the way we wanted it to be. It took us a few days to get our home straight. We did have electric lights, but cooking and heating were with coal, the living room fire having a back boiler to supply hot water. The bath was in the big kitchen, with a wooden cover which we used as a second table.

Edwin wanted to know where he would be going to school, and as he was now twelve years old his education was very important. Mrs. Hanbury was of help here; she phoned some schools and found one for him in Ware. It appeared that he could catch a bus from Dane End, a fair-sized village in the valley a little over half a mile from Green End, into Ware each morning and return to Dane End after school the same way. Green End, which is on the top of a small hill, and Dane End together make up the parish of Little Munden.

Dorothy and I visited the school which he would be attending and were pleased to be taken around the school by the headmaster and to talk to some of the staff. We felt sure this was right for our elder son, but we also had to consider John, who was three. He was growing into a very active boy, so the fear we had for him was receding, or so we thought. John was playing happily on our small lawn one afternoon when somehow our garden gate was left open; when we looked out to see if he was all right, he was missing.

We knew he could not have gone far, and Dorothy quickly found him. He was standing in the middle of a pond playing with the water and duckweed. Dorothy tried to get him to come to her, but her pleas induced no movement from him. In the end a man passing by enticed him out with some blackberries, and his mum had him in her arms in seconds.

She ran the 100 yards or so to our house, took off his wet clothes and wrapped him in a towel before attending to her own wet clothes. Mrs. Pearman, the farmer's wife, had seen the boy in the pond and had also come to get him out, but his mum had reached there first. I had not seen these happenings myself, as I had gone the other way looking for him.

Mr. Pearman came over later to make sure all was well. He stopped to enquire how we were settling into our new home and how I liked my job, when somehow cricket was mentioned. I learned that the field just behind one of our garden walls was the local cricket field; it looked miserably unkempt, as it had not been used for cricket since the beginning of the war and was just a field for Mr. Pearman's sheep, but he said there was a movement afoot to restart the cricket team. Would I be interested?

A meeting was arranged at the village school to try to restart the Little Munden Cricket Club and to enrol members and players. I was invited to join, and of course I did. Working parties were arranged to prepare the ground and to repair and paint the pavilion at weekends. All went well until a Saturday in May when the BBC was showing the Cup Final on television. Ken Smith, the new cricket captain, remarked that he was going to watch this football match and asked "Anybody like to come?" His remark was answered by a general putting down of tools, and we all clambered into cars to go the two miles to his farmhouse to see this new miracle, television, which few of us had ever seen. The screen was only twelve inches wide, but that mattered little to any of us, and we found it exciting to see these pictures in someone's home; most of us only had radio, so this was a new experience.

One evening when we were working on the cricket field the subject of Bridge was somehow raised, and Ken asked if we played. I had learned Bridge while living in a gardeners' bothy, and later, with two friends, Dorothy had soon picked it up. It appeared that most of the farmers in the district, farming at Dane End, Sacombe, Puckeridge, Benington and Datchworth, were somehow related, and each week they held Bridge evenings at each others' houses. Ken hoped we would join in to make up twelve people. Having made sure that Mr. and Mrs. Townsend would baby-sit for us, Dorothy and I were very happy to accept the invitation and, as a result, every third week we were hosts for these evenings.

At about this time Mr. Hanbury said he would like to show again at the Royal Horticultural Society fruit shows in London, which was something very close to my own heart. We had a good look at all our fruit, after which I had to agree that we could, and should, exhibit at these shows. Mr. Hanbury said that he would like to win a Hogg Medal, did I think we could do it? I promised to do my very best, and we agreed we could show at the July and October shows. The entry needed to be made by Mr. Hanbury himself, as the award only goes to an employer, though the prize money is paid to the gardeners.

The fruit was now of first importance, so we made another close inspection of the two apricot trees on the wall of my office block. Blackberries were also trained on a wall; strawberries, raspberries, loganberries and black currants were all inside a fruit cage, away from the birds. There was a small orchard of apples, pears and damsons, and a great many other fruits were trained on walls which could be netted when needed.

In addition to the preparation of fruit for showing, the production of vegetables and flowers was still of great importance, as was the care of the pleasure garden where cherry trees gave flower in the spring and the fruit was more than useful for our shows. Two of the trees were protected from birds by a wire cage supported by scaffold poles.

The grass at the base of one of these poles had grown rather tall, and there a pair of nightingales had built their nest. Mrs. Hanbury had noticed the nest, so a temporary fence was erected a little way off to stop people and animals going anywhere near. The adult birds sang most of the night, and also during the day, so it was little wonder that we wanted them to rear their young safely. One day when I was talking to the old gardener who had retired before the war, he said there had always been nightingales at Green End, even in his father's time.

The old gardener was such an interesting man; he had started his gardening living in bothy, where he had also learned bell-ringing, so he was able to tell me much about campanology. He had lived in the hamlet of Green End, spending much of his time in the little public house where Tom was the landlord. He, or his wife, opened the pub if there was a customer and closed it again when the last man left. They never gave time any thought!

In June a new Head Gardener took over the gardens of Dane End House, owned by Mr. Chancellor, who was a director of Reuters. I thought it right that I should go down to Dane End to see a fellow Head Gardener who was now my neighbour. Bill Brown and I became friends almost at this first meeting. He was a Scot whose only subject was gardening and where he had worked, so we soon found we had much in common. I invited him to Green End with his wife, and in a very short time there was real friendship between us. When he knew that I would be showing fruit in the RHS Halls in London he wanted to help, and I was only too pleased to agree. We exchanged visits frequently; I met Mr. and Mrs. Chancellor and, they knowing my employers already, a kind of partnership developed between the two estates.

Cricket had started in June, though I was able to play in only two games as I was so busy with the fruit shows in mind and with so much to do in the garden. Time was unimportant to me, so I was rather pleased when Dorothy told me that the Cricket Club had asked her and Mrs. Townsend if they would prepare the teas for the matches, if the club provided the food and the tea. I could see that the ladies liked the idea, and it would involve Edwin with the players. He had shown an aptitude for the game, and I was sure the men would not mind our John running around.

To add to their interests both the ladies joined the Women's Institute. I became involved in their activities, even if it was only talking at their meetings, and on these occasions Bill Townsend baby-sat for us.

In July we had to know what we would be showing, and to inform the Show Committee exactly which classes we would be entering. We were showing a collection of six fruits; in this class we put strawberries, peaches, black currants, cherries, raspberries and gooseberries. In the single-dish classes we could exhibit the same species, together with white currants, red currants and loganberries. We entered fifteen classes in all, in which each dish of fruits had to be named. After the judging, we found we had won a second prize for the collection; in the single dishes we were awarded five firsts, four seconds and three thirds. Everyone was happy with the results, but no Hogg Medal this time.

On the way home Bill said that he now knew a lot more about showing, and from now on he would be one of my opponents. I told him that I would welcome it, and would look forward to the time when he could compete.

Just outside the garden was an old pig-sty. Bill Townsend suggested that he and I should try keeping pigs as we could get plenty of left-over food with which to feed them, and it would help with the rations. Bill knew of an abattoir in Stevenage, and he would make inquiries. We bought two nine-week-old piglets which we were to keep for eight months, then the abattoir people would collect them, keeping one for expenses; we had the other one as bacon.

As we were unloading these two piglets, one escaped and ran out into the cricket field. We thought we could get it without much trouble, but that was our big mistake: catching a young pig is very difficult as it can run very fast and turn very quickly. This little fellow kept four of us fellows running, and at times falling over, trying to hold it. I suppose it was rather funny for Dorothy and Mrs. Townsend watching, but we weren't laughing. At last, when we were out of breath and the pig, too, was almost giving up, we were able to catch it and return it to its companion in the sty.

The July show was just a memory, I had to turn my mind to the later show in October. We now had to put the still-maturing pears into small cloth bags tied to the trees to protect the pears from the birds. Why they attacked this particular fruit I never understood, but just one peck and that fruit is ruined as it soon rots.

Living as we did in Hertfordshire, hornets were often troublesome. A nest was seen inside one of our sheds, attached to the inside of the roof. I was able to obtain cyanide on my Poison Book, if signed by me or Mr. Hanbury, but I now had the problem of getting the cyanide into the nest, so we used a stepladder which had a platform. I thought the height of the steps might bring the platform very near to the nest, but fortunately it was just about right. I put some of this deadly poison very near to the nest, sprayed it with water, then used a long stick to punch a hole into the nest, and ran quickly away, knowing that one sting would be very painful; many could be fatal. The next day all was silent, so we could destroy the nest and the grubs in it.

About a week later I was called to the pub, where they had a hornets' nest behind the pub sign, fixed to the wall but about three inches from the brickwork. This nest, being over the door into the bar, was a real danger to people going in or out. There was only one way we could approach and this was from a bedroom window which opened above the nest. I could put the cyanide right on top of the nest, a little water and a good poke with a stick, then quickly close the window. I thought it wise to tell Tom not to use the room that night. By the next day the nest had been destroyed.

In September Mr. Hanbury had to send in our entries for the October fruit show to the RHS. We decided we could enter thirty classes, for which staging was on the day before the show. Bill Brown was present and so very helpful, as was Bill Townsend. We took all our boxes by train from Ware to Liverpool Street, where we hired two taxis to Vincent Square, this time in the Old Hall. We staged five collections of fruit, twelve dishes of cooking and dessert apples, six dishes of six varieties of dessert apples, six dishes of six varieties of cooking apples, six dishes of six varieties of dessert pears, and three dishes of dessert plums. We also staged eighteen single dishes of apples, pears, plums and damsons, in all fifty-one exhibits. A dish of apples and pears was six in number, plums and damsons nine. Mr. Hanbury came in to see just what we were showing; he seemed very pleased with what he saw. After judging, we had gained eleven prizes from twenty-seven entries, six being first prizes, which we considered to be quite good, showing as we were in the premier fruit show. When we returned home Mr. Hanbury produced some champagne, but I still had no Hogg Medal for him.

In November the Ministry of Defence asked Mr. Hanbury if he would give employment to three German prisoners of war for a short time. He came to me with this request, and we agreed that we could do so after we had seen just what work we could give them and under what terms of employment. We were assured that we would not be responsible for their security. They would be provided with packed lunches, but we were asked to provide coffee or tea. We were told by the lorry driver who brought them that to get the best from them, cigarettes would help. I was relieved to hear that one spoke English fairly well; he seemed to be their leader and spokesman.

They did some hedging, ditching, digging, soil-mixing, general cleaning and leaf sweeping. We gave them coffee at lunchtime, and Mr. Hanbury supplied twenty cigarettes each day. We got along fairly well, owing mainly to Carl who explained our wishes to his companions. Before the war Carl had been a surgeon, and I'm sure he would have been better employed in a hospital. He said he must be careful not to damage his hands as he knew he would be repatriated some time.

While in prison camp he had made a small wooden inlaid tray, rather like a draughts board, with the inlaid squares of two different woods, and with raised sides. He said he wanted to give it to a friend, and I was that friend. I did protest, but I can remember him saying "Can't you be my friend?" After that I accepted, and took his hand. They were with us a little over two months, and then we did not see them again; I hoped they had gone home.

The winter turned very cold, so it was necessary to keep the greenhouse boilers running late into the night. All went well for several nights, then one night we had a breakdown when a section of the boiler burst and flooded the boiler room. In the glasshouses the temperature was rather low, so the breakdown must have occurred in the early morning. We collected together all the oil lamps and one heater, then I got the fire going in our sitting room and opened the windows of my house for the heat from our room to escape into the adjacent greenhouse. It was into this greenhouse that we quickly moved any plant from the other greenhouses which might be damaged or even killed by the cold. Two more oil heaters from the mansion kept the one house comfortable, but it was very congested with so many plants. We had the boiler repaired within the week, and the steps we took ensured that little damage was caused to the plants.

February is often a wet month, and that year was no exception. Living as we did on a hilltop, we took little notice of the extra rainfall. Edwin went to school as usual by bus. He would normally be home in the late afternoon, but one day he had not returned by teatime, and the afternoon post had not arrived either. Dorothy suggested that I go down to Dane End village to make inquiries. When I got there I found that the road had become a river, and the little stream which flows through the village was a torrent of water.

It was getting dark when I heard young voices and saw a group of schoolchildren coming towards a little gathering of parents. The youngsters had come across fields on higher land for over a mile when their bus could go no further along the road. They were happy and in good spirits, seeing no need to hurry! I was glad to see Edwin, one of the party, a bit wet and muddy but with no harm done. It appeared that not too much damage had been caused to the village, though later Bill Brown told me that part of his garden was flooded until late the next day when the stream became just a stream again.

Mrs. Hanbury asked me one day if I knew anything about beekeeping. Years before I had helped my dad with his bees, so I knew a bit about bees and still had an interest in them. She said she would provide everything I might need if I would care for them. We made inquiries with the local beekeeping society, and a member came to see me and asked where we intended keeping the hive. He gave me a great deal of information, then offered to set us up with a small swarm of a little under five hundred workers and a queen.

Having obtained everything needed to keep bees, with his help we made a beginning in June. He brought the swarm and I watched him hive them, which was most interesting. He told us we would have to feed them with sugar candy for one whole year, by which time we should have a good strong hive. I learned a great deal from my beekeeping friend which I would have to put into practice at a later date.

The cricket team was by this time playing two, or sometimes three, games each week. I managed to hold a place in the side most games. What pleased me greatly was that Edwin was taking a much more active part, and with my wife and Mrs. Townsend doing the teas and being in the Women's Institute, we were being accepted as village people. I was able to help in the school gardens, talking to the pupils at times.

My garden being my main interest, perhaps I spent less time than I should in village affairs. I had to consider my staff, who responded to me by doing the actual work very well indeed, giving me more time to organise the running of the garden and, to some extent, the estate. I was able to give much attention to this year's soft fruit show, starting as we did in the previous autumn, pruning, spraying to a set programme, tying and training wall fruit, changing soil where necessary, feeding, mainly by manure, testing the soil for lime content, and covering up trees in the event of frost.

That summer we had more nightingales singing, so we liked

to think that our protection of the nest the previous spring had paid off, although no one had seen the young ones flush. These birds were joined by thrushes, blackbirds and many other species, so it was a year to remember. Our hive of bees were certainly getting stronger. In July we looked into the hive and found quite a lot of honey, but our friendly bee man would not take any; we had to leave the honey as food for the bees that year. On looking carefully at our fruit, I thought our prospects for the soft fruit show were fairly good; our hard work was paying off. We had kept a watchful eye on the weather right up to the week of the show, and when we were picking and packing Mr. Hanbury was well pleased with all our efforts. Bill Brown was not ready to show yet, and he and Bill Townsend helped me with the travelling and staging; we went by train and taxi to Vincent Square. We entered twelve classes and, after judging, we had three first prizes, two seconds and two thirds, but the real success was a Hogg Medal for Mr. Hanbury. This award was for our collection of fruit.

I was asked to judge locally at Ware, Sacombe and Watton-at-Stone flower shows. True, it interfered with cricket, but it was a pleasure to go along as one met other gardeners, not only professionals but also amateurs, who can teach us a good deal, if we listen and watch how they do things. As professional gardeners we gleaned some knowledge in our training, but many amateurs can teach us a lot. That is the pleasure of going to local shows. I was also invited to give talks, mainly on gardening, at meetings of various local organisations. Once again, at question time one could learn much. One evening I was talking about the cost of nitrogenous fertilisers, only to be told that the content of an electric shaver, after shaving, is as good as any such fertiliser one could buy, and it was free!

That year, as we had two boys, we thought we would try one of those holiday camps, a new idea which seemed to be taking off. We booked in at the Hayling Island Camp, on the South Coast near Portsmouth, which turned out to be very good. Edwin and John, being of different age groups, had a grand time with young people of their own ages. We had arranged to meet Dorothy's brother Jack and his wife Nan, with their daughter and son who were nearer Edwin's age. It turned out to be the start of a family gathering. We were all pleasantly surprised at how well mums and dads were catered for, so we decided we would do the same another year and see if Dorothy's sister with her children would join us. It became the pattern for a few years.

The Little Munden Women's Institute held a garden party, by invitation, in our garden. I was rather pleased we had used begonias, geraniums, phlox and marigolds in the beds. The roses were still quite good, and the herbaceous borders showing a lot of colour. The ladies spent some time in the greenhouses, asking many questions. It was the edible passion fruit which intrigued many of them.

One day, I had a real problem. A swarm of bees emerged from our hive and gathered on a branch of a tree, so I rang our beekeeping expert and he told me how to proceed. Having dressed up in my protective clothing, I was to get the skep (a round straw basket about eighteen inches in diameter and depth) and hold it under the now hanging swarm, which I could reach by standing on some steps. Then I had to shake the bees into the skep.

When I had got most of the bees inside the skep I had to place it upside down on the ground, slightly lifted on one side to allow any flying bees to join the others. If the queen was there the bees would stay with her. My friend said he would come the next day to put the bees into our spare hive, together with brood chambers and shallow frames. He duly did this by putting a wooden platform, about two feet square, with one edge very close to the hive entrance and giving the skep a sharp 'bump' on to the platform. The bees all came tumbling out on to the platform and, to my amazement, all started walking into the hive. Then came the explanation; the queen does not fly unless she must, and will always take the easy way, the bees staying with her. I was also told that she does fly when she is mating, which takes place in the air, after which all she wants is a place to lay her eggs. I asked the expert about the hive from which they had come; he said there would still be a good swarm left and they would have made a new queen. He looked into the hive and found another queen cell, which he removed, as the bees would now make more honey for their winter feed.

For many weeks we had been preparing for the October show at the RHS, which would be much as before. The big difference this time would be that I would be in competition with my good friend Bill Brown. We held no secrets from each other; I had seen most of what he would be showing and he had seen most of mine. Bill was still asking questions, and seeking my opinions on his exhibits. He knew I would be as honest with him as he was with me, but when it came to the show benches no quarter was likely to be given.

I had just started staging at the show when I saw my father. We embraced, then he told me he was showing in a number of classes, so he would now be in competition with me, Bill and all the others. I wanted to know why he had not told me before, and he said this was to be his surprise. It certainly was that! All three of us were quite pleased with the results; I had won ten prizes, Bill eight and my father nine. After the show there was much to discuss, with a glass in hand, but the best result of all was Dad inviting Bill to Salisbury to see his two gardens.

Mrs. Hanbury and Mrs. Chancellor prepared some of the decorations in the church on special days. A great deal of this was achieved using a short ladder and steps, which is where Bill and I came in useful to the ladies who, along with other parishioners, provided and arranged the flowers for Christmas and other festivals. All this made our church very popular with visitors, much to the satisfaction of our Vicar.

In May, it was time for John to go to school. He seemed happy enough to go, but his mum was not looking forward to the day. Dorothy took him to meet the teachers and the other children, and when she returned home I went to see how she had got on, and a few tears were shed. Now that there was no child in the house, with both boys at school, it was all so very quiet. The afternoon, when she would once more have John at home, couldn't come quickly enough for Dorothy. When she did meet him after school he had a big smile on his face; he had been happy with the other children, and that was enough to put the smile back on his mum's face.

Bill and I met up with my dad at the Chelsea Flower Show as arranged. We had an excellent day together, the exhibits being, as usual, superb. The stands of firms like Suttons and Carters, showing mainly annuals, were a mass of colour, new designs everywhere, new plants to be seen in England for the first time, the use of water in the impressive rock gardens, and the colour in the vegetable stands was quite unexpected. The science section had to be studied, showing how and why things are done and giving an insight into gardening in the future.

It had been a bright, rather cold day, and in the late afternoon there were signs of a frost, so we decided it might be wise to get home as soon as possible. We stopped first at Bill's garden and covered his strawberries with the straw put there originally to keep the fruit off the ground, then we went on to my garden and did the same. After that we covered the potatoes with more straw, by which time it was almost midnight. My dear wife made us a hot drink and something to eat.

Bill started on his way home but soon came back, asking us to go with him a little way down the hill and there, in the moonlight, we saw the spectacle of frost rolling over and over down the hill. It is the one and only time I have seen this happen.

Bill showed against me in the July show, which was his first soft fruit endeavour. He did very well, as did I, but no Hogg Medal for Mr. Hanbury this time. When October came, Bill and my father also exhibited; for my part, I had my best ever returns, including a Hogg Medal for my employer.

I was beginning to feel that I had been in this garden long enough, and that we would go on doing much the same things every year. Dorothy, too, thought we might do better for our sons if we were nearer to a town. Edwin was doing well, and soon he would be leaving school; John would need a better school than this small one at Little Munden. I contacted the seed firms again, and kept a watch in the *Gardener's Chronicle*.

Tyntesfield 7

TWO MONTHS had passed without any word coming of a new position when I received a letter from Lady Wraxall, of Tyntesfield, saying she needed a real Head Gardener. I knew that Tyntesfield had been a leading garden in Somerset, and I was interested to know if that was still the case, so I wrote for more details.

By return I was asked if I could replenish a garden lacking leadership, and would I care to go for interview? I was met at Bristol by the chauffeur, and when we arrived at Tyntesfield Lady Wraxall was waiting for us. She and I first looked at the pleasure gardens around the mansion, which were in fairly good condition. The kitchen garden and the glasshouses were a few minutes walk away. There was a lot of glass, all in good repair, mostly quite modern lean-to steel houses, on walls facing south and west in a run of over six hundred feet, then came three sixty-foot span houses. At the east end of this area stood a large orangery.

There were two potting sheds, two fruit rooms, an open shed, a Head Gardener's office and a boiler house on the south side. These buildings were all of brick and formed the south-facing wall of the kitchen garden, making with the three other walls a square of about an acre. Again, on the south-facing wall was another steel peach house with five trained trees inside, then outside this garden was yet another peach case housing two more peach and nectarine trees. There was very little growing under all this glass, but the kitchen garden had been fairly well looked after, with some plants growing. Lady Wraxall took me into the three-bedroomed garden house; it was unoccupied, yet in very good condition, and quite spacious.

We went back to the mansion and, over a meal, discussed how best to get the whole place in production again. Lady Wraxall said she would put up some money to go commercial and so help

The main entrance of Tyntesfield, an estate near Clevedon in Somerset to which Arthur Hooper moved in 1950.

keep this large estate a paying proposition. Much was already happening on the forestry and maintenance side of Tyntesfield. She would not in any way supervise, that was in the hands of the estate agent who was not available that day, which would give me time to consider the situation and to return at a later date to see and talk with him.

The estate agent had an appointment in London and asked if I would go to see him there, which I did. As a result of that meeting we moved to Tyntesfield, having given Mr. Hanbury one month's notice. Before we left Dorothy was presented with a mantelpiece clock by Green End Cricket Club as thanks for all her wonderful cricket teas.

Dorothy was well pleased when she saw the garden house, and when we had moved in we set about getting our chattels in order. Edwin would soon be leaving school and the outlook for a good situation or training in a big city like Bristol seemed excellent. He continued his education at Nailsea Secondary Modern School for another six months before leaving to become an apprentice carpenter in Bristol with a company called Thomas & Co.

John had only been at Little Munden school for less than a year when we moved to Somerset, but within a matter of days he was in the local primary school at Wraxall. When Dorothy took him to enrol at the school she met the teachers and came away with a good impression, so we were happy for our young son. It was about a mile to the school, so my wife took John every day and met him later to bring him home. This continued for some time, but he was growing up and soon wanted to go to school on his own. He went by bus, the penny fare taking him to the school. Mum often found a reason to go to the village to see that all was well. There was no doubt this protective feeling was still with us; having lost one child, no way were we going to lose another. We made sure John never knew of this dread. He grew up, like his brother, doing his own thing and being independent.

I spent part of my first morning helping Dorothy get some order in our new home. When Bill Wines called and asked if he could be of some help, we were pleased with his assistance and from him we gathered more information. Lady Wraxall was a widow who was trying to keep the garden going until her son, now Lord Wraxall, who would be in the army for another three years, could get his discharge. Bill Wines and one other man, Tom Single, were employed in the glasshouses and kitchen garden, while Bob Monk and Ted Finch had care of the pleasure gardens.

Later that day Lady Wraxall came to see that all was well and to meet my wife. The two ladies spent a little time in our house, then Madam and I went to see the estate agent to discuss more details. If we made a showing of success I was to employ another man, or perhaps two more men, as there were still some empty houses available. It was also agreed that money would be arranged to purchase other equipment as needed. I was to see the agent each Friday morning, when he would give me the money for the wages.

Feeling happy with these arrangements, I could set about restocking the garden. Getting in touch with my many garden friends, I was soon receiving plants, but mainly cuttings, of chrysanthemums, geraniums, fuchsias and hydrangeas. There were some other plants I bought for stock, and seeds of particular species which I knew I would need when I started marketing with Bristol Wholesale Market. I would also need a foreman who could manage the garden in my absence. Keith, the agent, could see this was important. Asked if I had someone in mind, I told him I would appoint Bill Wines, who would be paid an extra five shillings if he wished to accept the appointment.

Bill was ready to help me, and said he would never let me down. His wife came into the garden to show her appreciation, and said she could help in the garden at any time. With so much pricking off and all the planting I had in mind, I was sure she could be of assistance.

With Bill as my foreman, I could spend some more time in the pleasure garden, where there was plenty to be done. Irish yews are not self-supporting, and an avenue of these trees was almost prostrate on the ground. The twenty-four trees would require a considerable length of wire to hold them in a standing position, and a Bristol junk shop supplied the answer with two one-mile drums of faulty telephone wire. Bob and Ted helped me to get these yews back into shape, and we had completed only a few when Lady Wraxall came along. Seeing what we had done, she expressed her happiness as she had not expected to see the avenue rise again, as she put it. She decided to stay with us to see how it was done, expressing her thanks when she left, after arranging to see me the next day on the terrace garden.

The terrace garden was a wide area of lawn, with large flower beds, protected by a balustrade on the south where the ground level fell away. A wide gravel path on the west side led to a one-hundred-year-old cork oak tree. On either side of the path were semi-standard holly trees only five feet high, each having a round clipped head. There were ten different varieties of holly in pairs across from each other, which was repeated once, making forty

The avenue of Irish yews which Arthur supported with two miles of old telephone wire. When he arrived at Tyntesfield he found the trees almost prostrate on the ground.

trees in all, a shrub garden a little way off from the path on the right, and a lawn running down to the Irish yews on the left.

A wide road led up to the courtyard and front door of Tyntesfield House. There were trees, underplanted with shrubs and bulbs, on the left and the Church on the right as one approached the rather lovely mansion.

Much as I would have liked to spend more time around the 'big house', I had to get back to my office and concentrate on production on the market garden side. Two span houses were prepared for cucumbers, fifty plants in all; many lettuces were to be planted in the peach house borders; there was room in the lean-to houses for some two hundred tomatoes and a great many bedding plants, seed of some already sown. I hoped I was doing the right things, but I needed more information, which I felt could only be obtained in the Bristol market. I spent two days in the market talking to growers and salesmen, a lot of that time with a Mr. Arnold, the director of Arnold Limited, who agreed to take my produce on trial for one year, with a further option. I had seen the method of packing flowers, fruit and vegetables; the time had been well spent.

Next I visited some of the growers in the Nailsea valley, who were quite happy to help a 'new boy'. After all these visits I felt confident to proceed. However, no longer could we do most things by hand. Keith, our agent, supplied the money to buy two Rotavators, a small one for use in the glasshouses and a bigger one for general use. Now we could prepare some land behind my house to plant about five hundred Christmas trees; with this machine the kitchen garden would be productive with much less labour.

I obtained my two-year-old Christmas trees from Sid Talbot, the Head Forester, who told me to wire them around because of rabbits. We did this, not knowing that we had interfered with a badger run. These animals promptly cut the wire, probably with their teeth. The answer was to put a kind of 'cat flap' in the fence on both sides, then all was well.

On a fine evening, the sunsets at Clevedon were remarkable owing to the dust in the air from the coal mines in South Wales. The sinking sun was a fiery red reflected in the waters of the Bristol Channel. Many people gathered to watch this spectacle, and sometimes we could watch the very high rise of a thirty-foot tide. Mum, John and I had many happy hours at Clevedon clambering over the rocks, while Edwin would be with his own friends. Edwin was still keen to play cricket, so he and I joined the Wraxall Cricket Club, where he was soon playing in the young side and doing very well. I had a few games but was more useful to the club as an umpire. Dorothy and John came to most matches, there meeting more people. We were once again village folk.

One of the players, one Jimmy Neate, was a member of a cider business. His father was complaining that no longer was anyone planting cider apples. We had some land at Tyntesfield which seemed to me to be wasted, so, knowing Long Ashton Research Station was nearby, I arranged an appointment to see the director with a view to planting cider apples. He was very helpful and said he would be interested in planning an orchard if we decided to proceed. Lady Wraxall, our agent and I decided that the twenty-acre field between the garden and Tyntesfield Camp could be so used if the Long Ashton people agreed. Tyntesfield Camp was a disused wartime American hospital, now the home of some thirty families.

The orchard was to be planted with two-year-old single-stem trees in double rows, fifteen feet apart and the same distance between the trees, then a gap of thirty feet, giving room for a tractor and sprayer in the years to come. First, we put in a cane where each tree would be; having got that right, we knew how many trees we would need for delivery in the autumn. Long Ashton told us to train our trees to a delayed open centre. Each tree should produce four or five branches about four feet from the ground, then three or four more branches two or three feet above the lower ones, the centre growth then being removed. This was to be done by notching, which meant taking out a small piece of bark just above a bud where we would like a branch to form. The sap moving up the stem would be checked at that point, encouraging the bud to grow into a branch. Where we did not need a branch, the small piece of bark was removed from below the bud. In most cases this method worked, but not always.

Mr. Arnold was quite pleased with the way we packed our flowers, vegetables and salads, which were selling well. So far so good, but I wanted to produce more, as I was getting ten per cent commission on all sales for me and the men. I had seen an advertisement in *The Grower* for a new kind of glass tunnel. A representative of the firm came in answer to my letter, bringing with him several two-foot sections of a tunnel with supports five feet high. The tunnels could, he said, be supplied to any length, with a spray line inside for watering. He also showed me a sectional glass frame for easy moving, two feet high, of any length as with the tunnels, and a glass end section. I was very impressed.

I knew that Lord Wraxall would be home that weekend, and I wished that he too could see these glass tunnels and frames.

When he, with Lady Wraxall and the agent, saw the value of these new ideas in glass they decided to invest six hundred pounds in the project. That gave me three tunnels of ninety feet, and a hundred-foot run of frames. The Dutch had recently introduced an autumn fruiting strawberry for which the new frames proved to be ideal; a new chrysanthemum called Loveliness, in pink, bronze and yellow and which only grew to three feet high, was just right for the tunnels. I had to buy in stock of these plants to propagate and later to plant under the new glass.

I was spending a lot of time building up the marketing side of the garden, but the grounds around the mansion were not being neglected. Lady Wraxall did her own flower arrangements in the house, so I spent a little time with the cook and Mr. Lathey, the butler. He and I became good friends, mainly because Mrs. Lathey and my Dorothy had so much in common. The Latheys had no children, so Mrs. Lathey became almost a second mum to our John.

One day Mrs. Lathey came to see me in the garden, and I could tell something was wrong as she could hardly speak. We went into my office but, as she was very distressed, it took a little time before she was able to tell me the problem. It seemed that the cook was making Mr. Lathey's life intolerable by not leaving him alone and wanting his love and attention all day, every day. He told his wife that he would leave Tyntesfield to get peace somewhere else.

Poor Mrs. Lathey was in a bad way, and wanted to know if there was anything I could do. I felt I could, perhaps should, try and do something for my friends. Maybe I did make a mistake when I said I would try to do something, but then she seemed a little more relaxed. That evening Dorothy and I talked over the matter and she, too, thought that I should try to help our friends. I asked Lady Wraxall if I could speak to her about a very delicate matter, and we retired to her little office. I had to tell her the whole sad story, and she thanked me for trying to help, saying she would attend to the matter. Two days later the cook left Tyntesfield.

Head Gardeners are often asked to carry out public duties, so it was no surprise when I was asked to talk at a Bristol Rotary Club meeting. Judging at local flower shows was a very pleasant duty; I think as gardeners we enjoyed being in demand for garden-related occasions, but when it became my turn to be chairman of the Bristol Gardeners' Society for a year it was a little daunting as most of the members were professional gardeners. I did have a problem during my tenure, as some of the members were unhappy with the treasurer. It was a tricky situation, but after much discussion he obtained a vote of confidence. By that time I had been taught a great deal about the running of a meeting, so when I was later asked to chair the Wraxall Cricket Club there was no problem at all.

The Bristol Chrysanthemum Society held a show in the autumn, and I entered a few classes with some success. In time I became a member, but I took no office as I could not spare the time from my garden.

One day Lady Wraxall invited me to join her and Keith, our agent, for a visit to a garden near Cheltenham. Keith drove as the chauffeur was unwell. We were about halfway to our destination when the car broke down. We had recently passed a garage, so Keith walked back for help and they duly came and towed us back to their garage. Clearly it was going to be a little while before we would be able to continue our journey, so Lady Wraxall asked for the loan of a car because we were now running late. This was arranged, and we were able to continue our journey. I spent a very pleasant time with the Head Gardener, who was also involved with market gardening so we were able to compare notes. I think we did help each other to some extent.

We had a meal in the 'big house' before embarking on our return journey, and when we arrived back at the garage we found that our car was ready. The cost of repair and the hire of another car came to £9 15s. Our lady carried no money, so she offered a cheque, which was refused, whereupon she asked Keith if he would settle the bill for her but, unfortunately, he also carried no money.

Now my lady had a problem. I asked her if I could help. She

was most surprised when I produced ten pounds, asking me if I could really afford that amount. I was able to say that I had no need of it myself at that moment, and she accepted with many thanks. When we arrived home we went to Keith's office and I was reimbursed immediately. The following day her ladyship came into the garden with a bottle of port for me and, going to my house, she left chocolates for Dorothy and the children.

By the end of the first year our sales had covered the cost of our glass tunnels and frames, which was considered satisfactory. However, so far labour costs had not been covered, though I was sure this would change very soon. Production was improving and sales returns were steady, tending to rise, so the outlook was encouraging. We had no plans to have a shop in the garden, but we found that people were starting to come in wanting to buy fresh vegetables and salads. It was here that Mrs. Wines, who was doing light work in the garden, was so very useful, adopting the situation as her own.

Some players of Bristol City Football Club came along, not only to buy but to ask questions regarding their own gardens. I gave them what time I could spare and, in return, Dorothy and I, with young John, had free tickets to watch some of the games at Ashton Gate on Saturdays. However, now that Edwin was playing football in a junior league on Saturdays, our spare time was divided between professional and amateur football, and watching our son play was the more important. Many Sundays were spent at the Bristol Zoological Gardens, the curator of which was also a member of the Bristol Gardeners' Society. I sometimes judged with him at local flower shows, as I did with others of the twenty or so judges from the society during the summer and autumn shows.

In 1952 King George VI died and Princess Elizabeth became our Queen. In due time there would be a coronation and I must consider growing many more flowers, anticipating a surge in demand, although at that time no date could be given. I had to take something of a gamble as to what to grow, though the timing was not entirely guesswork, as it was usually at least twelve months before a monarch was crowned, which would bring us to the spring or summer of 1953.

My wife, a forward-thinking person, was of the opinion that we should have one of these television sets that so many people were buying, hoping the BBC would cover such an important event. Having an aerial erected and payment for the set came to £79, an awful lot of money in 1952, but seeing the happy faces of my two sons and their mum, I felt it was money well spent! The pictures were quite good, but to get the best effect the light in the room needed to be diffused.

I had propagated the autumn-fruiting strawberries and had over two hundred plants fruiting in the glass frames. When I tried the market with twenty-four five-ounce punnets, Mr. Arnold rang me to know if he could have more, selling at eight shillings a punnet or perhaps even more. Over the following ten weeks I sent in over one hundred punnets, the price holding at eight to ten shillings, which encouraged me to increase my stock for another year.

The tunnels, too, were in constant use, almost full with lettuces, late peas, late carrots and chrysanthemums. We were growing five hundred chrysanthemums in large pots, which were housed in the orangery and greenhouses for the autumn and winter months when they would come into flower. In October we had sent into the market many boxes of cucumbers and even more lettuces. Mrs. Wines had graded boxes of tomatoes, and she was very good at packing flowers. The market prices had kept steady, and the time had come to consider getting a larger van. Keith, the agent, said he would see what could be found. Lady Wraxall must have been informed of our activities because she came to say how pleased she was, then requested a taste of the autumn strawberries. Not only did she get some of these but she also had some of the late peas and carrots.

She came to express her thanks, but she also wanted to see me on another matter. She was giving a party for her younger son Eustace, which would start on the Friday evening and go on until Sunday evening. There were to be many guests and sleeping would be a problem, so she wondered if my wife would help with the changing of the beds, perhaps up to midnight. I was not to pressure her in any way, I was to consider my family first. She put it to me this way, "If you will give me your permission, I will ask your wife myself". I considered this to be the mark of a real lady.

Dorothy did help when asked, and Edwin had the job each evening of lighting the many candles in coloured glass jars placed around the garden. He was to be given freedom of the kitchen, until he could eat no more! On another occasion when I did something which did not please her ladyship, she just said "I did mind a little". That was the hallmark of real class. She was a lady, always ready with praise, never giving an order, always a request, which would be carried out with pleasure by everyone.

We had been having a lot of trouble with grey squirrels damaging young trees, destroying many birds' nests and eating the eggs, so a winter squirrel shoot was arranged in the district. Each party consisted of four men with guns and three more with long telescopic bamboo rods. These were to prod each dray, usually high up in the trees, so that any squirrel hibernating would jump out, whereupon the guns would aim for a kill. We had been doing quite well until Lady Wraxall came along to see how things were going when, for some reason, our shooting was quite poor and some squirrels escaped. Her ladyship said "I think my absence would be appreciated" and went on her way.

The most important day in 1953 was 2nd June, the day of the Coronation of our new Queen. Like most people who had a television set, we arranged to have a party. My sister from Swindon would be among our guests, and Edwin's and John's friends would make up most of our viewing party, with their mums and dads, who with us supplied eats and drinks for the day.

The television coverage, in black and white, of course, lasted most of the day. In the morning we saw the many preparations on the streets of London and in Westminster Abbey itself that led up to the great event. The crowning itself was so very impressive, it being something none of us had ever seen. The young Queen, in a dress embroidered with all the national floral emblems of the

United Kingdom, appeared to be very calm throughout the proceedings, which lasted a long time, with much pomp and ceremony. Later, the appearance of the Royal Family on the balcony of Buckingham Palace drew a vast crowd, as we could see on our television set.

I had some benefit from the Coronation: the flowers which I sent to market sold very well. As I was now a grower of cider apples, I received an invitation to the annual cider tasting at Long Ashton Research Station during which all new vintages of ciders produced by the cider makers were sampled by over a hundred interested people. If they recommended one or more samples, then that cider would probably be produced for sale to the public. Talking to growers and brewers, I gleaned much more information about the varieties of cider apples which make up the many ciders we enjoy, and as a result I could understand the reason why the Long Ashton people had recommended the varieties we had

The garden walk and the house at Tyntesfield; the shadow across the foreground is that of a cork oak.

planted. Since these trees have a life span of a hundred years or more I could only hope we had planted for the future.

I was delighted when I heard from Bill Brown that he had accepted the Head Gardener's situation at Berkeley Castle and we would be able to resume our close friendship. We had always met at the Chelsea Flower Show, but now we would be able to visit the Wildfowl Trust at Slimbridge and Westonbirt Arboretum together with our families. I had never seen Berkeley Castle, but when I did I was most impressed by the castle, round and very tall. Those high walls needed the support of a series of buttresses, about forty feet apart, which provided little growing areas facing all aspects. In the south-facing ones were planted the tender species, whilst in those facing north were the most hardy plants. On the east and west aspects were to be found plants which were particularly suited to those conditions. This garden was unique owing to the structure of the castle and to its history over the centuries.

At the Bath and West Show I was most intrigued to see a block-making machine which pressed soil into two-inch cubes, with an inch depression in the top. Into these one could prick off one seedling or sow a single large seed, such as runner bean or sweetcorn. We were growing early and late lettuces by the hundreds, pricking them off in trays, then planting them in our glass tunnels and frames when they were still quite small, taking some weeks to mature. If they were pricked off into soil blocks they would be much larger at planting time, thus they would hold an area of ground for a shorter time, perhaps giving an extra crop on that site.

Then I had another thought: would I need to plant them at all? Why not just place them in a two-inch deep drill, then push the soil back with one's foot? I had plenty of room in our greenhouses for the early stages, and spraying them with water once a day would be no problem. I explained to our agent the advantages of the block-making machine, and he agreed that we should have one. The £52 investment was repaid during the first year, and that was not all; there was also a saving in man-hours at planting time.

We, like all gardeners, were troubled by rabbits. They were so plentiful that we had to wage something of an ongoing war to protect our plants. Things changed very rapidly when myxomatosis spread across the country. Myxomatosis is a very contagious disease; the rabbits suffer a great deal, their heads becoming enlarged and distorted, their eyes closing and their mouths dribbling. They seem to come above ground, maybe to breathe more easily, and they are only able to move short distances, until they can move no more and die an hour or so later.

It was painful to see these little animals, who must have been in great pain themselves, lying around. The most humane thing to do was to end their suffering; it is not an easy thing to do to kill a helpless animal, but we had no choice. It was not as if there were only one or two, either, there were so many on our estate.

Fortunately several men volunteered to help and they disposed of over one hundred bodies. For a time the road from Portishead, passing by Tyntesfield, was closed as the many dead and dying rabbits on the road were a danger to traffic trying to brake on the steep hill. The devastation of the rabbit population was almost complete, some years passing before we saw wild rabbits again.

Later in 1953 Lord Wraxall obtained his discharge from the Army and came home, and it was not long before he took over the estate duties from his mother. It took him a little time to adjust to civilian life, and for a time he expected us to carry out his wishes at once and quickly, though he did settle down. Maybe Lady Wraxall had some influence with her son, but even so he was impatient at times, which was not always to his advantage.

He had planned to have shooting parties in the autumn. The bracken on the hillside where they would be shooting was rather tall, so a pathway was needed for the use of the guns, and he asked me if my Rotavator would do the job. It would, of course. We loaded the machine on to his trailer and drove to the bottom of the hill. I cut a narrow path up the hill, but in doing so I encountered solid rock near the surface and decided not to rotavate down. The machine out of gear, I took a longer but easier route down. Lord Wraxall said he would rotavate up to make the pathway wider, then

The stone-built garden house at Tyntesfield which was home to Dorothy and Arthur for seven years.

he thought that to save time he would rotavate down. He started to go down, but the machine lurched forward when it hit a rock. He completely lost control, the machine tumbled over once or twice as it fell and was damaged rather badly. When he saw the damage he just said "Well, we will just get another", so a further £250 came off my market income.

He did have an interest in the estate and the market side of the garden. He noted the seven-foot-wide border in the lower peach house, which could be rather cold at times, and wanted to know if this border could be put to better use. The problem was the three winter months, because the peach house was not heated. The rest of the year it was in full use when the sun gave warmth to the house, so I really could not give my employer a satisfactory answer.

I was a member of the Royal Horticultural Society, so I was entitled to use their research information. They advised me to consider an underground electric heating system in the peach house. I went to Long Ashton Research Station to see this working, and thought it might solve our problem, though the cost would be considerable, having to install a transformer and then wire the ground. The wires needed to be four inches below the surface and about five inches apart for the whole length of the border. I could not see this as a viable project, and our agent was of the same opinion. However, when Lord Wraxall saw a demonstration he was very keen and decided to install this rather new idea without considering the cost. For my part, I was very happy to have it installed, for I would see some income from it. Even though it never repaid the cost, as a system it worked very well, but to be viable it would have needed to be on a larger scale.

In 1955 our son Edwin was twenty years old and he completed his apprenticeship as a carpenter and joiner. Within a week he was called up to do his National Service for two years. That was the order of the day. Those young men had no choice, so we had to wish him the best of good fortune for a time. John was now eleven and was getting very good school reports on both his academic and sports subjects. Dorothy and I were well pleased when we knew he was above standard in mathematics and literature. He was coming to the age when he would require new equipment for the many activities at school.

I was well able to help from my commission on sales from the garden, which were over £3,000 a year. Lord Wraxall and her ladyship showed their appreciation with a bonus for me and my staff.

Lord Wraxall made me his representative at the National Farmers' Union. At first I was unable to understand why he asked me and not his farm manager, but it seemed he would not be involved and had declined the request, so I attended the meetings and reported back. I found by being with these men that they had an interest in market gardening as well as pure agriculture; from them I learned much, as well as gaining more friends. A number of the members were smallholders, forming a link between agriculture and market gardeners, much to the benefit of all. The NFU held many functions, but I could attend only a few of them.

Tyntesfield was my priority; the pleasure grounds were so important, as was supplying fruit and vegetables to the mansion. I relied on my foreman a great deal, and my trust in him was never misplaced.

The autumn returns for the strawberry crop had fallen as other growers had noted the price we had been getting, so a change of crop was necessary. I turned to early courgettes, a vegetable which was becoming more popular. From seed we raised enough to fill our glass frames, which were planted in early March, and it was May when we tried the market. Mr. Arnold phoned for me to suggest a price. I suggested four shillings for a pack of six, a price that remained steady all that spring.

In September I needed to know how many Christmas trees would be ready for the December market. I could supply Mr. Arnold with about three hundred Norway spruce at five feet and around one hundred at four feet, all with roots left on. With his other suppliers, he could handle that number between 7th and 12th December, and only on those five days.

Little did I know at that time that my life was about to change again.

St. Pauls Walden 8

IN NOVEMBER I received a letter from Mr. David Bowes-Lyon's secretary asking if I would be interested in taking over the garden at St. Pauls Walden in Hertfordshire. Mr. Bowes-Lyon was President of the Royal Horticultural Society, and to be his Head Gardener would give me a high standing among the RHS membership.

Dorothy and I now had much to consider. We were happy at Tyntesfield, having made many friends, but on the other hand Lord Wraxall had never really forgotten his army training and at times I was not at ease in his company; I had often wondered if I could be as happy with him as I had been with his mother when she ran the estate. We decided that I would write for more information and perhaps attend an interview.

It was unfortunate that Edwin was away at this time in Germany, so we could not ask his opinion, and John was a little young to appreciate fully what the changes might be, though we did tell him he might have to go to a new school. His schooling was very important to us, so naturally we wanted to know about the standard of education in Hertfordshire.

My interview with Mr. Bowes-Lyon took place in London. Having talked long and frankly with him, I was clearer in my mind as to what the situation was really like. Dorothy and I were invited to go and see the Head Gardener's house, and for me to see the garden. The house, originally built for a Dowager Duchess of Strathmore, had five bedrooms, two sitting rooms, kitchen, bathroom and games room. The floor of the entrance hall was tiled. There were two entrances, the front one opening on to a drive, the other into the kitchen garden. The curved main stairway was quite special, the second stairs having been for the servants to go to their rooms.

It was all very impressive, and Dorothy was very much taken with the spacious house. She thought she would be happy there if I felt the situation was what I wanted and the schooling was right for John. Fortunately we met the gamekeeper, Jim Last, who assured us that the standard of teaching in Hertfordshire was very high.

The time had come to make a decision so, having been assured that our moving expenses would be paid, I accepted the position and agreed to take over by Christmas. I knew it would be difficult when the time came to hand in my notice, which I would give to the estate agent who would inform Lord and Lady Wraxall. Lady Wraxall came to see me but, being the lady she was, she never pressed me to stay on; she expressed her regrets at my going, offered me her hand and wished me success. Then she called on Dorothy to wish her and the boys good fortune, again offering her hand.

Lord Wraxall wanted to know if I knew of someone who could take my place. Bill Wines, who had been my foreman, was the obvious choice, so I told His Lordship that no one knew the job as well as Bill, and he was put in charge when we moved away. We had time to say farewell to our many friends before I took up my new post a week before Christmas.

Once again, it took a few days to get our new home in order. The schools would not re-assemble until after the holiday, which gave us time to make inquiries of the schools in Hitchin, our nearest town. It was during those early days that a detective called on us, showing his identity card, and saying that he must know something about us as Royalty often stayed at St. Pauls Walden and we might at times be in contact with them. Having satisfied himself that we were English, as were our parents, with no police records, he wished us well and left.

The lawn on the garden side of the mansion gave way to three grass rides, of which the middle one was about twenty feet wide and some three hundred yards long, with a stone feature at the far end, and having a six-foot-high beech hedge on either side. The other two rides, going off at about thirty-five-degree angles, also

St. Pauls Walden Bury, owned by Sir David Bowes-Lyon. Queen Elizabeth the Queen Mother was born there on 4th August, 1900.

with beech hedges, were much narrower. The length of these hedges was about one mile in all; they were quite a feature, keeping their golden brown leaves until the spring. Winter sunshine would light up the foliage, giving a spectacular glow of colour. One ride led towards St. Pauls Walden Church, the other had a temple at the far end, both rides being some two hundred yards long.

The triangular areas between the rides were planted with many shrubs and groups of one kind of plants, some low growing, others of variable heights, making a garden of real interest. Carefully planted oak trees gave some shade, as did the flowering and unusual trees such as *Davidia involucrata* (handkerchief tree), *Arbutus unedo* (strawberry tree), *Catalpa bignonioides* (Indian bean tree), *Cercis siliquastrum* (Judas tree) and *Eucalyptus* (gum tree). On the left-hand side of the lawn and near the house was the rose garden, leading to a lupin area on the bank of the lake, which covered about an acre. There was an island on which were growing some twenty-foot-high seedling trees and a rather mixed undergrowth taking over from a planting of *Hypericum*.

There were four men working in this part of the garden, plus two in the kitchen garden and glasshouses. There were five lean-to glasshouses on the garden walls in what was called the production garden, which was a little way off from the mansion, situated near the road leading to the village of Whitwell. The production garden was a little over two acres, and it was here that we grew all that was needed in the 'big house' and for sale in the market. Now that I was selling direct to the public, we had a stall on Tuesdays and Saturdays in Hitchin market. It had not been made quite clear to me on interview that this was the method of marketing, but it was a change, and I could set my own price.

The garden was well stocked with plenty of soft fruit. On the walls were trained apples, plums and peaches, and there was also a small orchard of pears and apples outside the garden walls. We used a Rotavator to do the heavy work, but planting was carried out by hand. In the greenhouses we grew a variety of pot plants, mainly for the market, and some forcing was done under the benches. One greenhouse was given over to *Cymbidiums*, which were grown for cut flowers. Ours was the only stall selling these orchids, so in season sales were brisk. Each plant would produce three to five stems; on these stems would be eight to twelve blooms, which were generally used singly for buttonholes or in groups as in a corsage or bouquet.

I went to the market quite often in order to keep a watch on demand and prices, so that I would know better what was selling well and could adjust my growing to demand. One thing I did discover was that small bunches of *Cupressus* were wanted by florists for wreath-making, and I was able almost to corner the market for this type of foliage.

John had started in a secondary modern school in Hitchin but was finding his school work very easy. His head teacher had noticed that John was somewhat ahead of his fellow pupils, and asked us to go and see him. He told us that John should be at the grammar school and could have a place there if we, and John, so wished. This was more than just pleasing, it was our wish. At the start of the next term, therefore, John was at Hitchin Grammar School, where he would find the work harder, though that troubled him little, and the facilities were better for physical education and sport. We were ever grateful to his ex-head, as our son's future now looked to be very good.

Our other son Edwin, having completed his two years of National Service, was discharged in the early summer of 1957. We were so pleased to have him home, to a home which he had never seen. It took a couple of weeks for him to find a job to his liking in Hitchin. He could have made the journey to his work by bus but that did not please him overmuch, so within two weeks he had bought himself a car. He had driven a little whilst in the RAF, so passing a driving test presented no problems to him. Having the use of a car, Edwin soon made friends in the local motoring fraternity. Dorothy and I were only too pleased to meet these young people, and in a short time were able to enjoy the company of their families. Some of the young motorists were also cricketers, to our great pleasure.

My two sons and I joined the Whitwell Cricket Club, where I played a few games while Edwin quickly established himself in the first eleven, not only as a batsman but as an all-round player. His batting was improving with every game, partly because he practised a lot in the nets. By the middle of the season he was making runs frequently, so he was promoted to open the innings. One Sunday, much to our joy, he made his first century at Whitwell. A little celebration was the order that day! It also meant that the family was accepted in the village, and John of course would follow his brother. John was quite stylish when he was batting. He liked cricket but he was not dedicated, as was Edwin. His interests were broader in many ways, yet both our boys enjoyed playing football in the autumn and winter, whatever the weather, so Mum and I would get quite wet or cold, or both, watching them play.

On one occasion Edwin was to play football at an away game. Whilst waiting at the end of our drive for his transport, he put his kit down in the middle of the road. Unfortunately a car came down the drive and had to stop while Edwin removed his kit. To our great consternation and embarrassment, the Queen was driving! We heard no repercussions, but we were never able to forget that thoughtlessness.

In the latter part of the year Mr. Bowes-Lyon held shooting

parties. Jim Last, the gamekeeper, persuaded young John to join a group of beaters who would beat their way in line through a wood or places with thick undergrowth, driving any game birds to an open area where people with guns could shoot at the birds in flight. John enjoyed this activity as it was something very different for him to do, and it earned him a little more pocket money.

It was at about this time that Mr. Bowes-Lyon was given an honour; from now on he was to be addressed as Sir David Bowes-Lyon. Somehow this seemed to be very right; all the many activities in which he was engaged for the country and for the Royal Horticultural Society were being recognised.

The lake project which had been in Sir David's mind was now discussed in earnest. Sir David asked me if I thought I could remove the island as it spoiled the view of the water from the mansion windows. It was an operation which I knew would be beyond our capabilities so, after detailed discussions, I had to say that it would be impossible for me to undertake it as I had neither men nor equipment, nor did I have the experience. The whole scheme, therefore, was put out to contract. Three firms expressed an interest. I was asked to see the representatives when they came to consider what was to be done. Each of these men said that the water level would have to be lowered. The matter must have been in their contract letters. Sir David asked if we could drain most of the water away ourselves.

We made a close examination of the lower bank, or perhaps it was a dam, which held the water back to make the lake. We dared not breach the dam as the weight of the water flowing through would be unstoppable, and yet it was the only possible place we could use. I asked the water company if they would advise me how to drain the water away safely. Their representative first wanted to see where the water would go, and in what quantity. I was advised to make a small breach, about two feet wide, just down to water level. Some water would perhaps escape, then I was to lower the breach by not more than an inch each day. He had calculated the weight of one inch of water in a lake of that size and the pressure of that amount of water, and he was satisfied that the bank would hold. He came to see me for several days to watch progress, and I was more than pleased to have such valuable help. He told me that as the water level dropped and the pressure lessened, I could lower the breach a little more each day, eventually to two inches when there was little or no water left around the island. I needed to retain as much water as I could in order for the fish to survive. There was no way of knowing how many fish were left, but there seemed to be a great many. Quite a number did become stranded on the mud, and there was little we could do for them.

My instructor came to watch our progress from time to time, and when the island was clear of water he told me how to rebuild the breach, suggesting that I fill sacks with a heavy clay type of soil, and surround each sack by small-mesh wire netting. When these were pushed firmly into the breach and packed around with clay, the water side was covered with thin cement each day for four days, behind which were more sacks of soil, fairly large stones, brick rubble and barrows full of soil and turf. When our man was

Arthur shows members of his family the lake after the work of removing the island and refilling the lake had been completed.

73

satisfied that the dam would be quite safe for many years to come, we could cover the whole with turf to match the surrounding bank. Wearing waders to get through the mud, the contractors were able to get on to the island and, using a large oak tree a little way off as an anchor, they worked out the young trees on the island. In so doing, a major part of the island collapsed into the mud flats which the water had left behind. What was left they removed by means of a large soil-removing bucket pulled through the remaining soil by a winch. It was almost a year before the area was a lake again. When the job was finished, Sir David had a bill from the water company, but he said he was happy to pay this knowing I had received expert advice.

The gardens were open to the public at times, and I was surprised at the interest shown in our lake project. People wanted to know our method of reducing the amount of water. As the lake filled again, everyone could see in the now clear water the many fish of different species, some small, some quite large. All this work had taken up a lot of my spare time as well as a good deal of my working time. I could ill afford much time away from growing and marketing, yet time had to be found for some Royal Horticultural Society fortnightly shows and, of course, the Chelsea Flower Show, where I needed to meet committee members, knowing that to have contact with these men might be to my advantage.

When the Russians invaded Hungary many refugees made their way to England, and Sir David gave of his time to help settle some of these people. Three young Hungarians came to work for me in the gardens. For a time our only method of communication was by sign or example. Two of them had the same name, which did not help much; they were Latzio, the other was Zen. Being intelligent young men, it was not long before they had learned some English and could understand what I wished them to do. They were very good workers and, through work, we came to understand each other better. They lived together in what looked like a garden bothy which had a cooking stove and a fireplace in one of the rooms. The furniture came from the mansion, so they were reasonably comfortable. They were expected to look after themselves, and that is where my wife could now do a bit of mothering!

Dorothy spent a lot of time talking, getting to know them, and gradually getting to understand them, and they her. They were paid wages, so they had to get used to English money. They went to the village, wanting to meet people, and it was in the local hostelry that they made much progress with our language in quite a short time. This was so important to them, as at that time it seemed that they were likely to stay here permanently. After several months things seemed to settle down in their own country, and the lads wanted to rejoin their own families, as did many of their compatriots, so arrangements were made for them to return home. We had been made aware of them going, and it was surprising how many people came to St. Pauls Walden to wish them well. We missed these young gentlemen in so many ways.

One incident is not to be forgotten; when the lads had learned in some way of our Mothers' Day, they came on that morning to see my wife to give her a bunch of flowers. It was very special for her and, for that matter, for me. The fact that the flowers had come from my garden was of no consequence. The gesture had shown that these men had wanted to say thank you, and they did so in the only way they knew.

For the Christmas market of 1958 we worked extra time, making holly wreaths and decorations to enhance the income. Sir David and her ladyship were very pleased, as it seemed that the extra income was needed. The lady now told me that this higher income must be maintained every week, but I could not promise it, which did not seem to please her. I was then asked to see Sir David in his office before the end of the year.

When I did, he said the garden income must increase and, knowing that I spent much of my time in the pleasure garden, he suggested I attend only to the growing and market side of the garden. He and her ladyship would oversee the staff around the mansion, leaving me much more time for the production of plants, flowers and vegetables for sale. Seeing that I was not happy with the idea, he said it was financially necessary and he could see no other way.

I felt that I was being put under pressure to carry out my employers' wishes without regard to the agreement we had made when I first came to St. Pauls Walden, so I began to consider my future. I was now fifty years old; if I stayed here I would go on producing, just for sale, for the next ten years or more, without doing any real gardening as I had been doing up to now. Dorothy and I talked over the matter and agreed that I might have to find other employment, but consideration needed to be given to our two sons. We both knew that I could not continue as my employer wanted, so decided to advertise in the *Gardener's Chronicle* under my own name, giving a month's notice of resignation.

I was more than surprised at the number of replies, five in all. One in particular interested me, from a Mr. Barclay at Brickendon, near Hertford. I had heard of the garden when in the RHS halls, so decided to answer his letter to ask for more information. Mr. Barclay's reply said much about the garden, which was interesting. He suggested an interview if I so wished; I could go on any Friday, when Mr. Barclay would be at home. It was arranged for me to be met at Ware Station by Mrs. Barclay, who drove me to Fanshaws at Brickendon, where Mr. Barclay was waiting to interview me. The meeting was satisfactory to me; it was good to know that my predecessor had retired, not just left.

There were three men employed under the Head. Mr. Barclay said he wanted a Head Gardener to take charge of the garden as well as the thirty-acre estate, most of which was woodland. We walked around a very pleasing garden, going some way into the woods. He said that if I accepted the Headship I would have twelve thousand pounds a year, backed by his bank, to draw cash as needed for garden expenses. Then he told me that all he wanted was for someone to take over the gardens and woods, as he no longer wanted to be bothered with the estate. He just wanted to return home after a day in an office to enjoy the garden with his wife and friends and to leave the worrying to me.

We went to Brickendon to see the gardener's house. I said I

would take the position if my wife felt she would be happy in our new home and the boys could settle, John to continue his education at the local grammar school, which I was assured was almost certain, and Edwin to find employment in Hertford or Ware. It was arranged for Dorothy to go to Brickendon to view the house, and she liked what she saw, a large semi-detached property overlooking the village green, with buses each day to and from Hertford. The local railway station, Bayford, was situated about half a mile away, midway between Brickendon and Bayford. There were trains every hour from Hertford, some coming from Stevenage, to King's Cross in London, stopping at Bayford Station. The neighbouring village of Bayford had a Post Office and two shops. The family were all happy to make the move, so I accepted the situation, Mr. Barclay covering my removal expenses.

Fanshaws

IT WAS not until the following March that we moved into the house known as Greys, at Brickendon. We had to ensure that John's education was not interrupted and were pleased when he was given a place at Hertford Grammar School, now known as the Richard Hale School. Edwin continued his work in Hitchin for a time until he found a situation to his liking in Hertford and was able to rejoin us in our new home.

The private drive from Brickendon to Fanshaws front door continued through the woodland to Bayford Station, in places passing through an avenue of rhododendrons. The south front of the 'big house' overlooked a large lawn and sunken garden. On the right were two rose gardens, one containing old varieties, the other modern, something over six hundred in all. Behind one of the hedges bordering the rose garden, on the edge of the woods, was a dog cemetery containing the graves of all the Barclay dogs.

On the left of the lawn was the round summerhouse, having herbaceous borders on either side, with shrubs behind the borders. It was here that two mulberry trees grew which seemed to attract much interest, the fruit being gathered to serve with sugar and cream or to be made into a preserve. From here one entered the walled kitchen garden, passing the stables and coach house on the way. The coach house was being used for garaging, whilst the stables had become storage for furniture and the mowers. Built into one wall of the kitchen garden was the old gardeners' bothy, with the usual outdoor stairs to the rooms above. It was now used as the fruit room and potting shed, which opened into one of the five lean-to glasshouses.

The soil in the one-acre garden was easy to work, rather sandy, and all the plants were in good condition, including some old varieties of fruit on the walls, amongst which were apples

Tom Putt, The Queen and Ard Cairn Russet, peaches Violette Hative and Magdala, and greengage Reine Claude de Bavay, as well as some more modern fruits. The older varieties were of considerable interest; fortunately the old lead labels were still attached.

There was another garage, built in around 1905 with an outside boiler to heat the garage; the early motors needed to be warm before they would start. This garage was situated near the mansion, screened from sight just inside the woods. Through the woods, and on each side of the drive, were masses of daffodils and

Fanshaws at Brickendon in Hertfordshire, named after the family who had once owned the land on which it stands. Arthur formed a most amicable relationship with his employer here, Mr. Barclay.

snowdrops, and an unusual feature was forget-me-nots which had naturalised each side of the driveway.

Fanshaws had been built in 1881 by Mr. Henry Saunders, the name Fanshaws being derived from the Fanshawe family who once owned the land on which it stands. Viscount Fanshawe took over the estate when he married Katherine Ferrery, who was known as the 'Wicked Lady'. She is said to have dressed as a masked man, and to have operated by night as a notorious highwayman. Her ghost, some say, still roams the Hertfordshire lanes.

As I had a staff of only three I did not need to employ a foreman since I would be with the men most of the time. Percy Sanders perhaps had most experience; Fred Harding also was a person on whom I could rely; Ron Clayton, I was informed, would be leaving in order to improve himself, and Gilly was the factotum around the house and estate, spending part of his time in the garden.

This garden had quite a reputation in the district for its roses, and with a staff of three I knew we would be able to maintain the standard in the local horticultural world. Friday afternoons had to be kept free for me to meet Mr. Barclay, and sometimes his lady, and to walk around the garden and estate, keeping them informed of the activities I had in mind and of the natural changes in the garden as the seasons came and went. I would get to know my employer's thinking over a cup of tea or a glass of sherry in the lounge after our walk. These afternoons became very important the more I learned of Mr. and Mrs. Barclay, and they of me. It was a meeting of employer and employee, but in an atmosphere of friendship.

A series of eleven arches, about thirty feet apart, covered a path which went along the top of the sunken garden. Each arch was planted on either side with rambler roses, which were rather old and no longer covered the arches. I could not remove them and just replant with new roses because the ground would be what is known as 'rose sick'. One day when I was in the greenhouse looking at the fuchsias, I noticed four plants of a rather vigorous variety called Chang. I wondered how tall they would each grow if I reduced them to only two leading growths, and I wanted to find out. Still in their ten-inch pots, fed and well watered, with all side growths reduced to two leaves, I took them out to the arches and tied them in. They had made growth up to nine feet by September, and I could see that provided I could over-winter them in frost-free conditions, we would be able to have fuchsia arches within two years. The greenhouses would be too warm for the plants to rest, and it was then that I looked again at the old heated garage. There would be enough light coming through the windows and I could get the old boiler working again for any bad weather.

That is exactly what we did, keeping the plants almost dry from November to March and supporting the long growths by hooks on the wooden wall. I was sure they would start to grow again in March, when they would need to be under glass, continuing to grow, until all risk of frost had passed. We took them out to the arches in late May as they were coming into flower. By mid-summer they had covered most of the arches and were in full bloom, as we had left the side shoots to develop. Cuttings of fuchsias root fairly easily, so propagating more for the remaining arches was no problem. My greatest pleasure came when both Mr. and Mrs. Barclay congratulated us on the new idea at Fanshaws.

I had been at Fanshaws a little over a month when Ron Clayton gave notice of leaving. He would be taking a single-handed job near Sandy. I rather wondered why a single-handed position, but he said he would be happy to be back in Bedfordshire near his wife's people. He asked me for a reference; as I had known him for so short a time I referred this matter to Mr. Barclay, who duly obliged. Now there would be a vacancy to fill, so I advertised in the *Gardener's Chronicle* and in the local press. A young man from Dr. Barnardo's Home came to apply for the situation, but I had to say that I was looking for a married man to live in the now-vacant house. A very disappointed young man left the garden. A few days later he returned, wanting to know whether if his mother would come to live with him, could he then be considered for the job. It was easy to see that he was very keen; he had reached eighteen and would have to leave Dr. Barnardo's Home. I wanted to employ this young man, for I liked his attitude, his good manners and his keenness to become a gardener, but I wanted to know something about his mother.

She was in Yorkshire, living in a caravan with a man who was not Robert's father. Robert told me that he had never known his father. I told him that he would have to be quite certain that his mother would come to look after him, and that she must write to me confirming her intention of coming to Fanshaws. In due course I received a letter saying that the lady would come, but then I learned that she had no furniture of any kind. Mr. and Mrs. Barclay and I gave the matter much thought; they said they would supply some furniture and were sure that their many friends would help, as did the Red Cross and Dr. Barnardo's, and so the house was adequately furnished for them.

During the few weeks before Robert's mother was able to come, he stayed with us. My wife got to know and like him, he was so helpful and polite in our home, later proving to be a first-class employee, so keen to learn. When his mother arrived I went to meet her and to help them prepare their new home. I was not impressed; she was untidy in her dress, and rather slovenly in her appearance. Though she seemed to want to help make the home tidy, she was never quite sure what was needed and where to put things. She always called me 'Sir' and gave the impression of being an unsure person. I could see that Robert was very much in charge, so I was hopeful that all would be well.

Some climbing roses on a trellis at the end of the sunken garden rather obstructed the view towards the summerhouse and borders. I decided to remove the trellis and lay the roses down, tied to wires supported by short stakes at a level of about a foot from the ground. The new growths carrying the flowers would look upwards and, being below eye level, would be seen better and the scent would be enjoyed much more easily. The advantage of having them raised from the ground a little was that we were able to hoe the soil underneath to control any weeds, and the flowers would not be splashed during heavy rain. I was sure that this would be a success as I had seen it done before. Then I had in mind to plant a border with clematis using the same method. I would need to select varieties which flowered from June to October and mingle them.

Edwin had joined a cricket club at Little Berkhamsted, a village about three miles away, and we were invited to go there to meet the cricket fraternity; we needed no encouragement. In a matter of just days the family was once more engrossed in cricket, as time permitted. It was a very good club, and the cricket was of a high standard, which might have been a legacy from Brian Johnston, who had spent his youth in the village and still had an interest in the club, always attending the cricket dinner.

The old pavilion did not do justice to the club, so it was decided to build a new and larger one. There Edwin's building experience came in very useful, so with him managing operations it was completed in a few months. We now had a bar, changing rooms and a lounge in which to entertain our guests.

We became involved in Brickendon village affairs when Mrs. Sanders, a parish councillor, invited us to help at the village fete. With approval from Mr. Barclay, we supplied not only manpower but also considerable garden produce. In doing so we became acquainted with most of the people in this small village. As we were living in one of the houses overlooking the green, we became partly responsible for seeing to the well-being of the green and helping in its maintenance. It seemed to be an unwritten law of the parish council's that the residents should help care for the green, while the parish council supplied the finances for the upkeep of this valuable asset.

A niece of mine together with her husband came to visit us as they were interested in gardening. I was escorting them around the garden one sunny afternoon, strolling towards the rose garden which had a sundial as a centrepiece, and as we approached to see the time, a cloud obstructed the sun. I made a silly remark, saying "Switch the light on". Toni, being a cartoonist, quickly fastened on to that as an idea. A cartoon in *Punch* showing a sundial with a light bulb above was the result.

The gardens of Fanshaws. Each Friday Arthur would walk around the gardens with Mr. Barclay discussing the work being done and the seasonal changes that occurred.

The Hertford Floral Society held a competition in the ballroom at Fanshaws which was well supported. The exhibits were of a high standard, and unsurprisingly my efforts came nowhere; neither did Mr. Barclay's and Barbara Cartland's. However, it was a pleasure to meet that lady and to converse with her. The show was well attended, but it seemed that what people really wanted was to see the inside of the mansion and to inspect the garden. I was very pleased to see the interest shown in the prostrate climbing roses, still in bloom at this late stage. People saw this as a new idea and asked many questions. The fuchsia arches also came in for a great deal of attention during what was a very successful day.

The days were getting shorter and cooler, so it was time to reduce watering and stop feeding the fuchsia plants from the arches. The water pipes in the old garage were once again filled, the boiler lit and tested. Now all was ready for the plants to start their winter sleep in November. Other fuchsias were still flowering; we needed them for decoration in the mansion until late in December or even Christmas.

Arrangements had to be made for the Christmas party. Many flowering plants were being grown, in the main chrysanthemums, poinsettias, cyclamen, hyacinths, and some narcissus. The party was for everyone, visitors and staff together. That was the plan, but we were called away as my mother-in-law was unwell. Mr. Barclay said they could manage, telling me to go and have Christmas with my parents and giving me a 'get well' card from him to my mother-in-law. Before leaving, I arranged the duty rota for the time I expected to be away. Fred would do the glasshouse duty and attend to the three boilers on Christmas Eve and Christmas Day, Robert on Boxing Day and the day after.

We all went to Salisbury on Christmas Eve. Mother-in-law had bronchitis, for which the doctor had given her some medication. She was considerably improved, so we were after all able to enjoy Christmas to some extent.

We returned home on the evening after Boxing Day and had just eaten when I received a message from Mr. Barclay saying that the house was cold, there was no hot water and did I know why? I went to Fanshaws at once, without stopping to change. My first stop was at the boiler room, where I found that both boiler fires were out, and had been for some time as the boilers were quite cold. I set about re-lighting them, but having to find some wood to start them the job took some time. Once they were going well, I went to the garden boiler which had also burned out, so there was another to light. I could not understand why Robert had let me down, and I was rather angry. It was now getting late, so I decided that I would see him in the morning. If I went to his house that night I felt I might have said or done something that I might later regret.

When I went into the mansion I saw Mrs. Barclay and told her what had happened. Mr. Barclay came along when he knew the problem. He told me to take what action I thought appropriate and said he would support me in anything I did, but the decision must be mine. The boys were in bed when I arrived home, and

Dorothy was becoming anxious as I had been away for so long. She was also concerned for Robert, hoping he was all right, and did I know if he was ill? It was a possibility, we would see in the morning.

Our day started at seven o'clock, but Robert did not report for work; now I began to feel that something was wrong. Having made sure that all the boilers were working and the greenhouses attended, I asked Percy to see to the needs of the house, then Fred and I went to see why Robert had not come into work. We found that the house was locked up and the curtains not drawn. There was no response to our knocking, so I assumed that the house was empty and Robert and his mother had gone away.

There was only a small toilet window not fastened, though there was no way we could enter by that means. After we had had some breakfast Fred and I, together with John, returned to Robert's house to try and find some way of getting in. It seemed hopeless, but I asked John if, with our help, he could get through the toilet window and go to the back door and unlock it, which he was able to do.

We passed through the kitchen to the living room where, to our horror, we found Robert still sitting in a chair, and obviously dead. He must have been dead for some time as he was cold and stiff. It took me a little time to realise what had happened, but then I thought about his mother. Where was she? She was not to be found anywhere in the house. John went to the telephone box to dial 999 for the police. He told them that one of my men had been found dead, gave them the address and asked for a doctor. They said they would be there in about ten minutes, and it would save time if someone could wait at the roadside to wave them down.

I asked Fred to meet them and I would stay with Robert. Two policemen came, a sergeant and a constable. After making sure that Robert was no longer alive, they said the body could not be moved until a doctor and a photographer arrived. They asked a number of questions about the deceased, and we told them that his mother should have been with him, but we had no idea where she would be. They went into every room and into the shed at the back, but she was not there.

At that point I asked Fred to go at once to Fanshaws to inform Mr. and Mrs. Barclay what had happened and to let them know that I was there with the police. I also wanted him to see Percy to tell him to attend to everything until I could get back to the garden.

I was given permission to go back home to see my wife to tell her the sad story, which upset her a great deal. Dorothy wanted to know everything, and decided to go and see Robert, but I had to say it was not a good idea as the police were there and would not allow her to enter the house. Having stayed with her for some time, I returned to Robert's house, as the sergeant had said I must.

The doctor had arrived and had examined the body, but although he could find no bruising or abrasions he was still not satisfied that it was a natural death. There was no gas in the house, but could he have had access to any poison, or poisonous plant? The sergeant ordered a search while he questioned me about Robert and his friends. During the search a small package was found with the words 'Poison' and 'Cyanide' on the outside. Seeing it as it was handed to the sergeant, I exclaimed "That's mine", which started a flood of questions.

I said "I will explain, if you will listen". There, on the package, was the supplier's name, Bentleys of Hull. I had bought the cyanide quite legitimately for fumigating the greenhouses against white fly and to destroy wasps' nests. It should have been in my poison cupboard, which was always kept locked. The cupboard was in the fruit room, which was also kept locked, so I had no idea how it came to be in Robert's house. The sergeant said that I was to accompany him to the fruit room to try and find out how and why the package came to be in Robert's possession. On arrival at the fruit room we found that the door was closed but not locked, and it looked as though entry had been forced. Inside, the cupboard door was open, the lock pulled away from its screws, probably with a nearby garden spade.

The sergeant spent a little time thinking, then he was satisfied

Dorothy sitting in the porch of Greys at Brickendon, the house she and Arthur occupied throughout the time he was working at Fanshaws.

that the spade had been used to force both locks. He said not to worry, but questions would be asked at a later date.

By the time we arrived back at the house Mr. and Mrs. Barclay were there wanting to be informed about everything—what I had done, what the police had done, what they intended doing, were Fred and I all right and had we been treated properly? They wanted to be fully in the picture.

The discussions went on until the body was collected, then the house was locked up. A little crowd had gathered outside, but I went home to Dorothy so that we could comfort each other.

Later that day the police came to ask if we knew where Robert's mother might be. All we were able to tell them was that she might be somewhere in Yorkshire, living in a caravan with some man, as she had been doing before she came to live with her son. We thought she might have returned to Yorkshire, which turned out to be the case when, after two weeks had passed, the police informed us that she wanted to come to the funeral and could she stay a night with us? The answer was a firm "no".

Dorothy said that she would not have this woman in her house, as we were sure that the whole unfortunate business would not have happened if she had stayed with her son instead of leaving him alone over Christmas. I was receiving much support from Mr. and Mrs. Barclay, who told me not to blame myself for the cyanide being taken from my cupboard.

When the inquest was held in February Mr. Barclay was concerned for me, and he engaged a solicitor to be with me. He would listen to the questions and, if he thought a question was in any way incriminating, he would ask me if I wished to answer. The problem never arose as the police evidence corroborated all that I had told them. The coroner wanted to see my signature on the poison certificate from the supplier, which Bentleys duly produced. The case was then complete.

It was well over two weeks before the body was released for the funeral, a time when we would have to meet Robert's mother again. Dorothy had a chance to say what we all thought, and told her in no uncertain manner that she was to blame for Robert's death. Now perhaps Robert could rest in peace.

In March I engaged Simon Judge to fill the vacancy. I felt I had to tell him and his wife of the unfortunate incident that had happened, rather than leaving them to learn of it by casual talk in the village. They were both happy to occupy the house, and Simon proved to be a very useful employee, one I felt I could trust with garden and boiler work.

We had raised more fuchsias for the arches. By June they were all in ten-inch pots and in position, so that by the time the garden parties were held the fuchsias would be in full bloom, causing much interest. The two rose gardens were a feature, responding well to feeding and spraying. The herbaceous borders around the summerhouse attracted much attention, or was it that refreshments were served from the summerhouse?

The holding of parties gave us all extra work, but our reward was a lovely colourful garden for everyone to enjoy, including the staff who, with their families, were invited to the garden on several summer evenings.

The seasons move on relentlessly. When the trees take on their autumn colours nature comes to maturity; fruit has been, or is being, harvested, the kitchen garden is giving of its best, some flowers have gone but many herbaceous plants are still in flower. The greenhouses are full of plants in their pots, many for the winter months and Christmas, such as cyclamen, fuchsias, begonias and chrysanthemums. Yet with all this wealth of produce, we must not forget the tender plants still in the garden; they will need protection or, as we call it, they need to be 'put to bed'.

The autumn so far had been quite mild, and of course plants respond. The roses had not noticed that the days were shorter; dahlias were still in bloom, rock roses started afresh, and abelias decided to keep on flowering, as did the clematis. The mild weather continued into December, but we had to think of the coming Christmas. Mr. Barclay and I went down into the woods to select a Christmas tree, which would need to be about twelve feet high, from our plantation. One week before Christmas we brought in the tree and set it up in the ballroom ready for decorating. Mrs. Barclay insisted that real candles were to be used, so Gilly would stand by with a bucket of water and a syringe. I thought that this was a bit hard on Gilly, but when I mentioned it he told me that it was something he always did.

On the afternoon of Christmas Eve I was in the rose garden looking at the many roses still flowering. I noticed that one variety, Sutters Gold, had quite a number of flowers open, or about to open. Making a rough count, I thought I might be able to put out a table centre of roses for Mr. and Mrs. Barclay and guests on Christmas

Day. When everyone sat down to Christmas dinner, there were forty-five roses in a bowl as the table centre.

On Christmas Day we were all with our families and, to give my staff a break, I carried out the boiler and greenhouse duty myself. I must have been noticed, for Mrs. Barclay came out to find me. I was asked to go into the mansion to meet the guests for congratulations on the table centre! It was all a little embarrassing, and I was glad to go home to my family.

Boxing Day started with the local hunt meeting on the village green. There were a few protesters, but it was a grand sight and everything went off peacefully, with the landlord at the *Farmer's Boy* supplying liquid refreshment to all who cared to visit his hostelry. The evening party for everyone at Fanshaws was a very happy affair. Everybody received a present from the Christmas Tree, and Gilly did his job by needing to do nothing.

The weather changed dramatically as 1961 came in, our Friday afternoon walk being somewhat curtailed, not only because of the weather but because Mr. Barclay was not very well at times. We hoped he would improve with the coming of spring. As the days warmed up he was better, but he attended his London office much less, giving me a chance to see and talk to him in the garden considerably more. Some of his enthusiasm seemed to drain away, so I decided not to make any major changes in the garden and our work became to some extent a repeat of the previous year, though there would be less activity as two of the July garden parties would not take place.

Our holidays had to be selected with care. Edwin was still with us, a qualified carpenter and joiner; John had left school and was training to be a mechanical engineer with an engineering company near Ware. It was August before we could get away. On our return I was informed that Mr. Barclay was very ill, then in a matter of days he died. Everyone was devastated, so sorry to lose him, as he had been a super employer in so many ways. I was able to see Mrs. Barclay to express sympathy on behalf of the garden staff, and at that stage she seemed unable to comprehend her great loss and, for that matter, the loss to everyone.

When I had gathered my thoughts, I realised that considerable changes would now be made. It was my duty to tell the men that I could no longer guarantee their jobs any more than I could be sure of my own. Simon told me that he had been offered a job in Dorset, which he had been about to turn down but would now reconsider as it seemed to be the right kind of situation for him. Percy and Fred said they would await events for a time, and as for me, Dorothy and I had discussed the position and decided to wait as perhaps it might be possible for us to remain at Brickendon. We continued to work in the garden, which needed to be kept straight until we received other orders, which would be most unlikely perhaps for several weeks. There was still money in the bank for wages, so I went to see the bank manager, who said he would release money for wages but for no other reason until further instructions came from the estate.

A surprise encounter 10

WHEN MR. Barclay was laid to rest at a very moving ceremony, a number of people from Barclays and other banks and his many friends joined with the family to say farewell to a lovely man. As Dorothy and I were leaving the church, a gentleman asked me if I would see him in the garden the following day, saying it was of some importance. He arrived in the afternoon, introducing himself as a Mr. Wallace, owner of Fanshaws!

I immediately thought he was trying on a 'fast one', telling him that the estate was owned by the late Mr. Barclay and that it would now belong to Mrs. Barclay or her family. Then, without being rude, I asked him to leave. He said he could understand my attitude, but please would I look at a document which he withdrew from his pocket? When I examined the document I saw that it was a receipt from Mr. J. Wallace to Mr. Barclay for one year's rent for Fanshaws, dated and signed. I still found it hard to accept, telling him that I would see the bank manager for confirmation.

Mr. Wallace said that he would be happy for me to do this, and would I please see him again two days later as he had a proposition to make. In reply I said that if I received confirmation of what he had told me, then I would be pleased to hear what he had to say. The next day I went to Hertford to see the bank manager, who confirmed that Mr. Barclay had never owned Fanshaws and had indeed rented it from Mr. Wallace.

Mr. Wallace came as arranged, knowing that Mrs. Barclay would be leaving Fanshaws and giving up the tenancy on the last day of September. The estate would then be put on the market in one or two lots which would include three of the five cottages in the village. The semi-detached houses in which Fred and I lived would be retained. He told me that Mr. Barclay had rented Fanshaws on a yearly tenancy, and he had given his word to Mr.

Barclay over twenty years ago that he would never ask him to move out. "I have always kept my word and always will," Mr. Wallace said.

He proposed that I stay on with my men to look after the estate until such time as it was sold. No one would be allowed to buy it unless they gave an undertaking in writing to employ us for one whole year, at the end of which we should do just what would be best for us and our families. "This is my word, will you accept it?" he asked me. I had no wish to leave Brickendon; both my boys were in good jobs and it was important for John to be able to finish his apprenticeship, so I accepted the offer for myself.

When I put it to the men, they also accepted. Mr. Wallace wanted to see me and the men together, when he offered his hand in good faith. We all shook hands as a promise to stay; it was something of a ritual but it did seal a trust which, for our part, was a relief.

There were a few things I wanted to know, and perhaps Mr. Wallace had some items to discuss because we arranged to meet a week later, by which time I would have a clearer idea how to proceed. Our wages would be the same, but our hours of work were reduced to thirty-six a week. We were to keep the boilers working, mainly in the winter months. Any produce from the garden would be shared between us, and we could sell surplus to have some money for necessities. Simon had accepted the situation he had been offered and would be leaving; I was pleased to give him a good reference.

There was still one thing which needed consideration: who now owned the garden tools and the two mowers which I would need? Mr. Wallace said they were the property of the Barclay family, and he understood that there was to be an auction of all items in the house and garden not wanted by the family. He would guarantee to buy all the tools, mowers, barrows, etc., if I would give him a list of my necessities.

Within a week of the funeral, with the help of Mr. Barclay's brother and his wife, Mrs. Barclay moved out of Fanshaws. Quite a quantity of furniture and private possessions went with her. She seemed to have been in a hurry and no one was able to wish her well, neither did we know where she went. The auctioneer lost no time in preparing for the sale, putting items into lots for his catalogue. When he came into the garden I thought he would want everything put into lots, but all he wanted was my hundred or so chrysanthemums in nine-inch pots put into groups of twenty and given lot numbers. Everything else had been bought by Mr. Wallace by private tender, all to be kept at Fanshaws or taken to his own garden at Datchworth. This arrangement pleased us as we would still have our plants to care for and the tools with which to continue gardening.

Many people came to the auction. The bidding was brisk, and in less than five hours everything had been sold. Much was taken away that evening, the remainder the next day. The few items which were not collected were stored away and kept for a jumble sale in the village hall a few weeks later.

The house was now empty; the butler had accepted a situation in Stevenage; the four Italian girls went to their embassy in London and we did not see them again. The rest of the domestic staff were local ladies, who for a time were not working. Mr. Wallace left it to me to keep a watch on the mansion and grounds.

The sale of Fanshaws went very sluggishly. It was not until the spring of 1962 that any interest was shown, although we did have one Royal couple and one other small group of visitors. In December of that year two gentlemen from The Institute of the Motor Industry showed considerable interest, wanting to know about the train service at Bayford Station. After inspecting the house, they wanted to know if the sewage system was in working order and if the water supply was plentiful. I was in their company for over two hours, and when they left I hoped they were happy with what they had seen.

It seemed, however, that they were not entirely satisfied. When I reported the interview to Mr. Wallace he said he would contact them immediately, but nothing seemed to happen.

Edwin had a lady friend whom Dorothy and I had come to know very well, so it was no surprise when they told us they intended to marry in the early spring of 1963. Arrangements had to be made, but Valerie's father said that he would take no part in any of his children's weddings, so Val asked if they could have the wedding from our house, with which we were happy. Her mother was very co-operative, and together with the two Mums, Edwin and Val organised things. Val spent some time with us making her own wedding dress.

Quite a large congregation gathered in Bayford Church for the wedding, the reception being held in Brickendon Village Hall. We were then able to meet all Val's brothers and sisters and some other relations. The young couple had no home of their own and would be living with us, as Edwin said, "For one year".

During that year we maintained the garden and estate in good order as Mr. Wallace had asked. He made a visit each week with money for wages, and inspected the house to see that all was well, and again later when we put the heating system on. It was obvious that he was a man of considerable importance, for he made no secret of the fact that he had bought many acres of land in Hertfordshire, Bedfordshire and Essex knowing there was a great deal of gravel below the surface which he intended to extract when permission was granted. His company, Redland, would extract the gravel, then the site would be used as landfill before being returned to its original use.

It was during one of these extractions that a large and somewhat mysterious object was found. Under Mr. Wallace's direction, great care was taken not to damage the find, which was eventually identified by experts as a Roman corn dryer. One Sunday morning a gathering of over a hundred people saw a most careful recovery. A wooden platform was carefully pushed underneath as the gravel was removed, then drying kiln and platform were carefully lifted by crane on to the back of a lorry on which had been placed a three-inch layer of sand to cushion against vibration during transport to Hertford Museum.

From time to time Mr. Wallace invited me to his home at Datchworth, sometimes taking plants from my greenhouses for his own use. He had a fairly large garden; most of the trees and shrubs were mature, and in some cases they needed to be replaced. Mr. Wallace asked me if I would advise his man, whose knowledge of gardening was limited. Alf was only too pleased to receive any advice I could give, he so wanted to stay with Mr. Wallace and work in his garden. To this end he would drive over to Fanshaws sometimes to watch us and learn how to run his garden.

It was during one of Mr. Wallace's visits that he told me he had received a request from The Institute of the Motor Industry for an inspection to take place of the sewer pipes, as they had not been in use for some time. It might mean that the pathway where there was a bend in the pipe would have to be excavated. A few days later three men came to dig up the path and then to inspect the pipe. When they reached the sewer they found that it was not a pipe, rather a small tunnel which when opened was found to be completely lined with glazed tiles. It caused much comment and many photographs were taken; the inspector said he had never seen anything like it in all his working life.

Percy Sanders had decided to concentrate on his hobby of grafting fruit trees and budding roses in his own garden, and wished to leave. I was not too unhappy about his going, since our workload was so much less, with the production only of plants and vegetables required for ourselves and Mr. Wallace.

In November Mr. Tipper, the Director General of The Institute of the Motor Industry, and Mr. Charles, the President, together with eight other gentlemen, spent a day at Fanshaws with Mr. Wallace. I was asked to meet the company to answer questions about the garden and estate, and also about the houses in which Fred and I lived. I escorted two of them to my home and showed them over the house and garden. They also wanted to talk to Fred and Gilly, inquiring about village life, about the local amenities, and wanting to know about the road and rail services, even where we did our shopping. It was obvious that they had come to see everything with a view to buying Fanshaws. When they had departed, Mr. Wallace said that he was fairly certain he had made a sale, and that our jobs would be written into the contract if the outcome was as expected.

December 2nd, 1963, was a very important day for us: our first grandchild, Brian, was born. He was a lovely healthy baby and Val, the new mother, was very well, and like us excited and happy. We contacted Val's mother, who was with us within the hour. Unfortunately Val's father did not come to congratulate his eldest daughter or to see the child. The arrival of a baby in the house meant there were changes, but I don't think the changes were even noticed, we were so happy.

Our joy of having this infant with us didn't last long as Edwin and Val were able to buy a house in Hertford. There was much work to do in the house, however, but Edwin was able to do most of it himself, and they took up residence in January.

Later that month Mr. Wallace informed us that The Institute of the Motor Industry had bought Fanshaws and would need our labour on a permanent basis. They would want us to remain in our houses, rent-free, whilst employed by the Institute. There was much activity in the mansion, with rooms being changed from domestic to office use. The servants' quarters were made into a lovely flat for Mr. and Mrs. Tipper and their daughter and the servants' hall became a canteen, but in the main the interior was changed very little. The grand ballroom and stairway remained intact, and the dining room was still a dining room.

On 21st April, 1964, Fanshaws was opened as the headquarters of The Institute of the Motor Industry by the Lord Lieutenant of Hertfordshire, who said "We who live in Hertfordshire rejoice in the fact that you have brought your Institute to Fanshaws, for by so doing you have found a useful purpose in the twentieth century for an abode such as this, together with its beautiful grounds, thus enabling it to remain in existence and to continue to maintain the beauty and peacefulness of our countryside which, through the force of circumstances and changing times, is so rapidly being broken up. May you prosper in your task of fostering and improving the techniques of this major industry, both nationally and internationally."

The following day a staff of about twelve moved in with Mr. Tipper, who escorted me into the various offices to be introduced

Greys at Brickendon; Dorothy and Arthur occupied the left-hand house, the other one being the home of the foreman.

to his staff. I was very pleased to see that two domestic ladies were back in the situations which they had had with the Barclays, and the cook, too, was reinstated in her old job, which was now renamed Canteen Manager. I realised that more produce would be needed from the kitchen garden to supply the canteen, but this would be no problem. It being April, there would be time to sow and later plant many vegetables.

On 30th December of that year our second grandson, Peter, was born. Dorothy and I lost no time in getting to Hertford to see the new arrival. Val was very well, and the infant was introduced to his year-old brother. John was once again an uncle, of which he was very proud. The new-born had presents from almost everyone in the two families.

During 1965 I had the pleasure of meeting many important people from the motor industry. They mostly had homes with gardens, and so were interested in the plants which we were growing. I was asked many questions on gardening and at times shown photographs, sometimes just so that I could admire their gardens, sometimes in order to identify plants. However, it was the trees which caused much comment; among these were our two mulberry trees, the huge *Magnolia grandiflora* which grew against the wall of Fanshaws, the smaller *Magnolia stellata*, and *Magnolia x soulangeana*. The *Cercis siliquastrum* (Judas tree) is of considerable interest in May, when the flowers are produced on the old, hard wood. The leaf structure of the *Gleditsia aquatica* (cushion locust) is a little unusual, as is the *Eucalyptus* (blue gum). I found it surprising that so few people recognised the *Carpinus betulus* (hornbeam), which is very widespread in Hertfordshire.

The Institute was very active and already needed more room, so the flat above the coach house in the stable yard was altered and modernised for Mr. and Mrs. Tipper and their daughter. When they moved in their flat was taken over by a new cook/housekeeper and her husband, who was a chauffeur. The stable block had been built on land known for centuries as Long Leys, which was the name chosen by Mr. Tipper for his new home.

In the summer of that year I became very ill with shingles, and for a time was unable to work. Maybe it was fortunate, for one day as I was at home looking out of the window at the trees across the village green during a thunderstorm, I saw a tree struck by lightning. It split the poplar from the top to the ground with a deafening crack; steam rose from the soil and debris was thrown around, and the house momentarily shook. It was rather a frightening experience. The sight of such a powerful event makes one feel very humble, and sad at the loss of such a beautiful thing as a tree.

During 1963 John had given us the pleasure of meeting Barbara, a young lady friend of his whom he had met at the company where they were both working, she as secretary to the Managing Director. In a very short time we could relate to her as she was very easy to talk to, with a pleasant smile. The young couple bought themselves a small van which gave them greater freedom, especially when John was playing football or cricket, or there was a meeting which they wanted to attend. We were able to meet Barbara's parents. Her father was an independent ophthalmic optician in the town of Ware and, being a Rotarian, both he and his wife were highly respected citizens.

The lower rose garden was planted with species, moss and Bourbon type of roses, which were getting quite old. Some of the members of the Institute were unable to appreciate their garden value and asked if I would grow something different. After discussions with several of the members, we agreed to turn it into a heather garden. Since there was much colour in the rest of the garden during spring and summer, I decided to plant winter flowering heathers, with a few dwarf, slow-growing conifers to give a little height. It pleased me to know that the members, when visiting, were taking a keen interest in the garden, making comments for me to consider.

A little before Christmas, 1965, John and Barbara told us that they planned to marry in the spring. It was great news for everyone, but not unexpected as they were engaged. Dorothy and I, together with Barbara's parents, George and Edna, had much to discuss about invitations to the wedding. They, with Barbara and John, would organise all the arrangements when they knew how many guests would attend the wedding, which was to take place at Christ Church in Ware. I suggested to Barbara that I would be happy to make her bridal bouquet, together with those of the two bridesmaids, an arrangement with which she was very happy. We discussed flowers, and I told her that as my *Magnolia stellata* would be in full bloom I intended to use it as the basis of her bouquet.

On the day, all the bouquets included flowers from the gardens at Fanshaws. The top tier of the three-tier wedding cake, which had been made and decorated by Barbara and her mother, was adorned with lily-of-the-valley from my garden. That was special too, because lily-of-the-valley was Dorothy's favourite flower and perfume.

When the great day arrived on 2nd April, 1966, a large congregation gathered for the ceremony and many came to the reception on that happy day. The young couple stayed with us for a time until they had found a house in which to set up home. In less than a year they were able to buy a house in the village of Benington with a garden at the rear.

One day when we were preparing ground outside the back door for a patio area a hand grenade was dug up. The police were informed and the Army Bomb Disposal Unit arrived to check the grenade and to search the ground around it for further ammunition. It appeared that it was safe and it was taken away, after which we could concentrate on the garden once more.

The gardens of Fanshaws, which attracted the attention of many people from the motor industry on their visits to the Institute of the Motor Industry.

I was pleasantly surprised to see how keen Barbara was to learn about gardening, though she already had some experience as her father had quite a large garden. Dorothy and I became very good friends with Barbara's parents and we spent much time together.

When Fred decided to retire and move out of his estate house I was presented with something of a problem, as I was now left with Gilly as my only helper. It meant that with a reduced labour force I could use only part of the kitchen garden. Mr. Tipper understood the problem; he said they would buy the food for the canteen and would at a later date consider the whole situation with his committee and myself. The time had come to consider my own situation. We were very happy living in Brickendon, and we had no wish to move. I was now in my late fifties, Dorothy and I were much involved in village affairs and in Little Berkhamsted Cricket Club, while Edwin and his family were living only a few miles away. John and Barbara were also fairly close. We decided it was almost out of the question to move, so we would stay on and I would see what I could do in the garden.

The day of the promised meeting arrived and, after some discussion, a proposal was made to let the kitchen garden and glasshouses. I was able to say that I knew of someone who was interested, if he could buy or rent the unoccupied house, and an interview was arranged between Mr. Tipper and Mr. Shadboult, the interested party. In due course, the matter was sorted out to everyone's satisfaction. Mr. and Mrs. Shadboult moved in as my neighbours, taking over part of the kitchen garden as planned. It made my task much easier, so all thoughts of moving were forgotten.

On 24th December, 1967, John's son, Robert, was born. Barbara and baby were well, and everyone was happy, particularly Barbara's parents as this was their first grandchild. Two days later Dorothy and I went to Benington to be introduced to the new baby and see the new Mum, who was a very happy young lady.

At Fanshaws, the peony border was now rather old and well

past its best, so a change was needed. I was allowed to employ an extra hand on a temporary basis so that we could widen the border and plant it with shrubs. I selected a wide variety including *Hydrangeas hortensis* and *quercifolia*, *Philadelphus* (mock orange), *Magnolia stellata*, *Hamamelis mollis* (witch hazel), *Cistus* (sun rose), *Ceratostigma willmottianum* (hardy plumbago), *Ribes* (flowering currant), *Olearia* (daisy bush), *Myrtus* (myrtle), *Hypericum* Hidcote, *Potentilla fruticosa* Red Ace and Katherine Dykes, and *Senecio greyii*. All these plants would be of variable heights and at their best at different times. Planting as we did in the autumn and winter, I was able to obtain snowdrops at their green stage to underplant some of the shrubs, in clumps. The heather garden was maturing and beginning to look good when in flower, brightening dull winter days.

Edwin had set up his own company in the dry rot and woodworm business, and seemed to be doing well. John had taken a job with E.R.F. Limited in Sandbach, Cheshire, to where he and Barbara moved in December, 1970. It was an important career move for John, but we were very sad that they had to move so far away. However, we were able to go and visit when George and Edna made the journey by road, inviting us to join them. I was able to help a little in their garden, though not with much success, as the soil was so difficult, being mainly deep clay.

On 1st April, 1971, Barbara presented John with their daughter, Andrea. The baby had some problems for a time but was soon thriving. It was some little time before I could go to see our only granddaughter, but Dorothy went to look after the family for a couple of weeks and I joined them all later.

One day at Fanshaws when I was mowing the lawn with my old thirty-inch Ransomes mower I was asked by a member to stop as he wished to examine the machine. I could see no reason why he should want to, but he spent some time looking and pondering, then remarked that the machine had only a single 1,000cc cylinder. He asked me if I knew the year in which it was made, but I didn't know, so he said he would find out. It turned out to be a pre-war model of 1938, still doing a grand job after nearly 40 years!

I had a problem of my own when Gilly became ill, passing away after a matter of only two weeks. It left me single-handed, and when I approached Mr. Tipper about a replacement he said it would be a matter for the committee to decide. The decision, when it came, was that there would be no replacement, I would be the only gardener. I was sixty-five; Dorothy and I talked the matter over and I resolved to retire.

The car at the door of Fanshaws might be seen as emblematic of its role as the Institute of the Motor Industry.

Retirement

WITH RETIREMENT looming we had to find a new home. Having no house of my own, I applied to the local council for accommodation. The council informed me that I would have to wait for a house to become available, but there was a flat vacant into which we could move straight away. We just could not live in a flat with no garden, so we decided to wait for a house, and it was eight months before we were offered a bungalow in the village of Hertford Heath in August, 1975. I accepted the tenancy and gave notice of my retirement, which was accepted with regret.

The Institute gave me a little retirement party, then we moved into a rather nice bungalow with a small garden and in very pleasant surroundings. Edwin moved us in September and helped us settle into our new home.

I was already known in Hertford Heath as I had been judging at their village flower shows for several years. The secretary of the Horticultural Society called on us to welcome us into the village, and asked me to join in their activities. I attended their next meeting, at which I was elected a member of the committee. Now that I had more time to spare I was included on the district judging panel for flower shows, gardens and allotments, which in turn provided more opportunities for public speaking. It soon became clear that I would be kept quite busy. Dorothy would be able to attend some of my engagements, which pleased us very much.

Haileybury College was situated at Hertford Heath, where the public were able to watch many of the activities, including cricket, rugby, squash and hockey. I had the good fortune to know a lady whose late husband had been employed on the sports fields, and she was able to invite us into the theatre to see the production of various plays. In the grounds there were some lovely trees; in the hollow interior of one old oak was a nest of bees which were known to have been there for over fifty years, as no one had been able to take their honey in all that time.

In spite of all my other activities, I found time to help Edwin with the many jobs he was engaged in. It was a very different kind of work, but I soon became used to spraying woodworm and cutting out dry rot. By that time John had moved from Cheshire to take up another position in Market Harborough in Leicestershire, buying a house in the village of Wilbarston, about five miles from Market Harborough. Dorothy and I were soon invited to see the new home which had a nice garden, though it was a bit neglected, which gave Barbara the chance to make the kind of garden she wanted. Between us we planned many changes, always leaving room for alterations at a later date.

My niece Ann and her husband Bob, with their son and his wife, were with us on 12th November, 1977. We were enjoying the day together and, in the early evening, Edwin, Val and their two sons joined us. Edwin and Val went off to a dance, while we sat talking after eating.

Dorothy asked to be excused and went to the bathroom. After a while, Ann said "Auntie has been there rather a long time, I'll go and see if she is all right". She rushed back to us, crying out "Come quickly, Auntie is on the floor". Dorothy was not breathing, so I applied artificial respiration immediately. Bob rang for an ambulance and a doctor, and then took over from me as I tired, then I relieved him again. We dared not stop in our efforts, and mouth-to-mouth resuscitation was little known at that time.

When the ambulance men arrived they took over from us until the doctor came. He made his examination, then said the two dreaded words, "I'm sorry". Dorothy was laid gently on the bed; I couldn't believe that I had lost my darling. The doctor, thinking to console me a little, said that she hadn't suffered even for a minute.

I remember the police coming, but I still cannot recollect my 'lovely' being taken away. Someone had telephoned John and Barbara; Edwin and Val called to collect the two boys, then I had my family with me which was more than a great help. Ann and her family returned to Southampton in the early hours, then I had to go to my bed. John wanted to stay with me, but I knew that I must be on my own, and must be on my own this very night.

John and Barbara had to return home to their two young children, but Edwin came back early the next day as arrangements had to be made with an undertaker, who took charge of everything. The doctor was unable to issue a death certificate, saying there would need to be a post-mortem to determine the cause of death.

When it became known that I had lost my wife many people called to express their sympathy. I found it very difficult to meet these people, as their kindness was at times a little too much. When the death certificate was issued the funeral could take place. I was told that many people attended the service in the parish church. Afterwards, we were taken to Hertford, where we left my dear wife of 43 years in the care of Mother Earth.

At a gathering in Edwin's house afterwards, Barbara said to me "Because of our Mum, you have four lovely grandchildren to care for and they for you". I don't suppose Barbara will ever remember those words, but they are deep in my memory; she was right. She was also very close to Dorothy.

I thought that I would be very lonely when I was on my own, but it was not entirely so because I had many engagements. All of my family invited me to stay with them for a time, which I did when I could fit it in with the activities I was asked to carry out in the horticultural world, including some interest in the grounds of Haileybury College.

Time passed well enough until the breakdown of Edwin's marriage. I had been aware for some time that things were not as they should be, even so it was something of a shock when Edwin and Val parted. The two boys were in their teens, so they were able to understand the situation. They stayed with their mother in Hertford, while Edwin moved to Somerset where, in due course, he married Pauline. I now had another daughter-in-law who should be welcomed into the family, but my close relationship with Val never changed. I went to Taunton to stay with Edwin and Pauline on several occasions, finding that I could care for Pauline. When little Vicki was born it gave me great pleasure to see my new granddaughter and to watch her grow up.

I almost surprised myself when I realised that I was eighty and some of my family descended on me with their presents. It was a very happy day; we had plenty to eat and drink, yet I supplied nothing.

I was still judging at flower shows and doing some public speaking, but it didn't come so easily as it had before, so for the first time I refused some invitations, well aware that younger people could do as well as me, or even better.

It was all brought home to me when I had a bad attack of bronchitis. I telephoned the doctor, who came and gave me a prescription, but when I asked him how I could get it made up, he said "That's up to you". There was nobody about, so I got up from my bed and went to the chemist in Hertford, encountering some difficulty getting home. I am sure John and Barbara would have helped had I telephoned them and told them, but I did not.

I felt that the time had come to consider my future. During the time I had been a Head Gardener some of the gardens were open to the public at times, and some of the income from entrance fees had been given to The Gardeners' Royal Benevolent Society. I knew they had a nursing home and sheltered accommodation in Sussex and elsewhere, so I broached the subject of applying to visit the home in Henfield with my two sons, who both said by all means go and inspect the home but remember that they had each offered me a home or, if I wished, I could stay six months with each of them every year.

However, the idea of being with other gardeners appealed to me, so I went to Henfield to have an interview with the Matron, Mrs. Painter, and I rather liked what I saw and heard. I made no commitment, because I needed time to consider with Edwin and John, but in due course I asked for another interview. This time I had a meal with the residents, spending some time in their company, after which I decided to take up residence when a room became vacant. Matron seemed pleased with my request to

In his retirement Arthur continued to take a great interest in gardening; he is seen here in the garden of Red Oaks at Henfield in 2000.

become "one of us", as she put it, and said I could go almost immediately as there was already a vacancy.

It is not easy to break up one's home, but having so much help from my boys, it did not present a problem for me. John and Barbara came to pack everything which I would need to take with me and drove me to Henfield where, with the help of the carers, I became a resident of Red Oaks in December, 1989. I shall always be grateful for coming into this home, where I have a lovely well-furnished, warm, clean, en-suite room with a comfortable bed. There are two lounges, one having television and one being for reading or writing. In the large dining room excellent food is served. The games room becomes an extra lounge, if needed, and the conservatory serves as a room for people who smoke. The nursing and care staff are always on hand and do a wonderful job for us. Quite often there is entertainment, and our own minibus makes frequent trips to gardens and other places of interest, or perhaps to the seaside.

We have a large garden growing plants for colour or for

special interest. This is important as we are all gardeners, mostly men but also two lady gardeners, together with widows of gardeners. In all there are just over fifty residents. The Gardeners' Royal Benevolent Society has homes in Sussex, Yorkshire and Scotland, plus sheltered accommodation in Cambridge, Sussex and Gloucestershire.

Since coming to live in Henfield I have made many new friends, not only amongst the other residents but also outside Red Oaks where I have been asked to take part in many activities. For a few years I was an umpire with Henfield Cricket Club, until it became too much for me to stand 'out in the middle' for several hours at a time, especially in very hot weather. I have continued to go and stay with John and Barbara each year for a short time, and in August, 2000, my friend Elizabeth and I went to Wilbarston to stay and to attend the wedding of my grandson, Robert, to Fay.

Edwin, Pauline and Vicki all made the journey from Taunton for that occasion and we were able to have a lovely family party, though there were some, like Dorothy, not present who would have very much enjoyed the occasion; Barbara's father had died in 1983, and Fay had lost both her parents. In spite of that, it was a wonderful weekend.

Elizabeth's two daughters who live in Sussex with their families have made me very welcome at their homes, which compensates just a little for my sons both living so far away.

Now the time has come to put down my pen; we are going in our minibus to visit the lovely garden at Leonardslee to see the wonderful collection of azaleas and rhododendrons.